Introduction

One of military aviation's first specialisations was 'Spy in the Sky'. The advent of fighters during the First World War rendered the use of tethered balloons and airships for reconnaissance/battlefield observation too risky. The answer was a new class of aircraft – scout aircraft in which the second crewmember, in addition to his main duties as a gunner, would photograph objectives in the enemy's rear area, such as airfields and garrisons. Safety from enemy attacks (and thus mission success) was ensured both by the defensive armament and by the aircraft's speed and altitude performance. The latter two became the main parameters for reconnaissance aircraft in the Second World War.

With the beginning of the jet age the speed and service ceiling of combat aircraft improved appreciably. For reconnaissance aircraft, however, altitude performance was of greater importance than speed because high-speed interceptors guided by ground-based air defence radars could easily catch up with the target and destroy it – which they found harder to do at high altitudes. A high-flying spyplane with high aspect ratio wings was harder to detect and engage, since interceptors tailored for high speeds usually had swept or delta wings that did not allow them to climb that high. The interceptor's armament, which added weight (and, in the case of air-to-air missiles, also added drag), was another limiting factor here.

After the Second World War the USA was the nation that attached the greatest importance to aerial espionage, launching the Peacetime Aerial Reconnaissance Program (PARPRO) targeted against the Soviet Union. This led to the development of such high-performance spyplanes as the Boeing RB-47 Stratojet, Martin RB-57, and later the famous Lockheed U-2 and the equally famous Lockheed SR-71 Blackbird. Later, when mankind started exploring outer space, this, too, became an arena for espionage activities, surveillance satellites being developed and placed into orbit. As for aerial reconnaissance, it was largely reoriented from photo reconnaissance (PHOTINT) to electronic intelligence (ELINT). The highly specialised sensitive equipment on board a 'ferret aircraft' allowed it to detect and identify enemy emitters (radars and the like), eavesdrop on enemy communications and even obtain high-resolution electronic imagery in real time.

The Soviet Union, too, developed and fielded a whole range of reconnaissance aircraft in the post-war years; yet these were not 'true' spyplanes, being intended for tactical tasks, not strategic ones. In the mid-1950s the Soviet Air Force did possess a small number of aircraft that qualify as spyplanes in the traditional meaning of the word – the Yakovlev Yak-25RV specialised high-altitude reconnaissance aircraft, the first of the kind in the Soviet Union. Unfortunately its career proved to be very brief and, unlike its US counterpart (the U-2), next to nothing is known about its operational use – both because of the small production run and because many archive documents are still classified.

In the 1960s, however, the Soviet 'fighter maker' Mikoyan developed the famous (and very capable) MiG-25 high-speed aircraft which had a number of reconnaissance variants. The story of the MiG-25R *et seq.* is much longer (even today the type is in service with the Russian Air Force) and much better known. Its capabilities and the missions it has performed over the years mean the MiG-25R qualifies as a true spyplane. Later the Soviet Union fielded a number of other ELINT aircraft. Yet for reasons of space this book deals only with the two abovementioned types.

MiG-25s at Neu-Welzow AB, Germany, in 1991 or 1992. MiG-25RBS '52 Red' is nearest, followed by MiG-25RBT '54 Red'. '75 Red' in the background is a MiG-25BM suppression of enemy air defences (SEAD) aircraft.

Acknowledgements
This book is illustrated by photos by: Yefim Gordon, Chris Lofting, Sergey Skrynnikov, Mikhail Sidel'nikov, Sanjay Simha, Dmitriy Komissarov, Sergey Burdin, Chris Dewhurst and the archive of Yefim Gordon. Colour artwork: Vasiliy Zolotov, Viktor Mil'yachenko. Scale drawings: Vladimir Klimov. The authors have referred to the following web sources: www.airliner-models.org, www.anigrand.com, www.armory.in.ua, www.gallery.rumodelism.com, www.karopka.ru, www.rumodelism.ru, www.scalefan.ru, www.scalemodels.ru.

'Soviet U-2'

The Yakovlev Yak-25RV

As early as 1951 the Moscow-based OKB-115 design bureau led by Aleksandr S. Yakovlev (*opytno-konstrooktorskoye byuro* – experimental design bureau) began development of an all-new patrol interceptor at its own risk. Such an interceptor with long endurance was desperately needed for defending the Soviet Union's Far East and High North regions where it would be difficult to set up a system of surface-to-air missile (SAM) sites. Bearing the in-house designation Yak-120, the aircraft was a two-seater (the crew consisted of the pilot and a radar intercept officer). It was a mid-wing monoplane with thin wings were swept back 45° and sharply swept cruciform tail surfaces. The powerplant consisted of two 2,000-kgp (4,410-lbst) Mikulin AM-5 axial-flow non-afterburning turbojets mounted in slender nacelles adhering directly to the wing undersurface. The chosen layout dictated the use of a bicycle undercarriage with wingtip-mounted outrigger struts. The interceptor featured the new and promising RP-6 **Sok**ol (Falcon) radar in a large parabolic nose radome and was armed with two 37-mm (1.45 calibre) cannons.

On 19th June 1952 the Yak-120 performed its maiden flight. The manufacturer's flight tests proceeded until November. While admittedly heavier than single-engined air superiority fighters of the day, the aircraft was smaller and lighter than its Mikoyan and Lavochkin competitors (the I-320 and La-200). Moreover, the Yak-120 surpassed the Air Force's specific operational requirement in all respects except range and endurance, which fell a little short of the requirements; even so, the aircraft was able to patrol an assigned area at a considerable distance from its home base. However, development of the Sokol radar was taking longer than predicted, and as the radar was unavailable the Yak-120 could not be submitted for State acceptance (= certification) trials. Hence in early December 1952 it was decided to fit the prototype with the less capable RP-1 *Izum***rood** (Emerald) radar as a stop-gap measure. From March to June 1953 the Yak-120 was tested with the provisional radar installation at the State Air Force Research Institute awarded the Red Banner Order (GK NII VVS – *Gosu**dars**tvennyy Krasnozna**myon**nyy na**ooch**no-is**sl**edovatel'skiy insti**toot** Vo**yen**no-voz**doosh**nykh seel*). Even though the State commission did note a few short-

comings, the general opinion was favourable and the aircraft was recommended for production under the service designation Yak-25. Production took place at aircraft factory No. 292 in Saratov in southern Russia, which turned out the first production interceptors in September 1954. Very few were built with the Izumrood radar. By the end of 1953 the RP-6 was finally brought up to scratch; in April 1954 the Yak-120 prototype successfully completed its trials, and at the end of the year the initial version was superseded in production by the Yak-25M (*modifitseerovannyy* – modified) featuring the new radar. The Yak-25 entered first-line service in 1954, followed shortly by the Yak-25M. Both varieties were allocated the NATO reporting name *Flashlight-A*.

The same directive of the Soviet Council of Ministers (i.e., government) and Communist Party Central Committee dated 10th August 1951 which formally launched the Yak-120 tasked OKB-115 with developing a photo reconnaissance version. The first attempts proved abortive – the Yak-25R ([*samo***lyot**-] *razved*chik, reconnaissance aircraft) and Yak-25MR never entered production, as they were already obsolete by the time they were tested. Yet, three years after its service entry the Yak-25 evolved into a very different aircraft – the Soviet Union's answer to the Lockheed U-2. In 1957-58 the Yakovlev OKB developed a strategic reconnaissance aircraft designated **Yak-25RV** (*raz***ved**chik, vy**sot**nyy – reconnaissance aircraft, high-altitude). Some early documents referred to the aircraft simply as 'Yak-RV'.

The Yak-25RV programme was officially launched by Council of Ministers/CPSU Central Committee directive No. 419-198 dated 16th April 1958. This specified a service ceiling of 20,000-21,000 m (65,620-68,900 ft), a maximum speed of 900 km/h (559 mph) at 15,000 m (49,210 ft) and 800 km/h (496 mph) at 20,000 m, a minimum speed of 750 km/h (465 mph) at 20,000 m, a range of 2,500 km (1,550 miles) at 20,000 m, 3,500 km (2,174 miles) at 16,000-18,000 m (52,490-59,055 ft) and 5,000 km (3,105 miles) at 13,000-14,000 m (42,650-45,930 ft).

Structurally the aircraft had very little in common with the original interceptor. Firstly, wing loading had to be reduced considerably to ensure good high-altitude performance. Hence the wings were all-new; they were unswept, with more than twice the span – 23.5 m (77 ft 1¹³⁄₆₄ in) versus 11.0 m

Opposite page:

The progenitor of the *Mandrake* – the Yak-25M *Flashlight-A* interceptor. The swept wings of relatively short span with boundary layer fences are readily apparent.

This view of the Yak-25M shows the AM-5 engines, the large nose radome, the two-seat cockpit and the twin cannons located low on the centre fuselage sides.

(36 ft 1⅝ in) for the Yak-25/Yak-25M, an area of 55 m² (591.39 sq ft) versus 28.96 m² (311.39 sq ft) and an aspect ratio of about 10. As a result, wing loading decreased from 310 kg/m² (63.55 lb/sq ft) to a mere 175-178 kg/m² (35.87-36.49 lb/sq ft) – less than that of the Second World War-vintage Yak-3 fighter!

Secondly, the thrust/weight ratio was improved dramatically by using a new power-plant. The interceptor's 2,000-kgp (4,410-lbst)

Mikulin RD-5A (AM-5A) turbojets gave way to Tumanskiy R11V-300 turbojets – a special non-afterburning high-altitude version of the R11F-300 engine powering the Mikoyan MiG-21F *Fishbed-C* light fighter (once again, the V stood for *vy**sot**nyy* – high-altitude). The R11V-300 delivered twice the power of the RD-5A – 4,000 kgp (8,820 lbst) at full military power and 3,250 kgp (7,165 lbst) at nominal power. The new engines required the nacelles to be designed from scratch.

Above: '75 Yellow', the first prototype Yak-25RV reconnaissance aircraft. This aspect shows clearly the high aspect ratio unswept wings with no fences, the 'solid' metal nose tipped by a pitot boom, the single-seat cockpit and the new R11V-300 engines in redesigned nacelles.

The forward fuselage was new, featuring a single-seat cockpit and a reshaped all-metal nosecone housing avionics and equipment; a vertical camera was housed in the rear fuselage. The tail unit was also redesigned, with slightly increased leading-edge sweep, a larger fin fillet and a variable-incidence tailplane. Changes were made to the landing gear: the outrigger struts retracted forward, not aft, and because of the narrow tip chord the wingtip fairings housing them appeared disproportionately large. The twin wingtip pitots were replaced by a single nose pitot. Finally, the Yak-25RV was unarmed, albeit the said directive had stipulated a single Nudelman/Rikhter NR-23 cannon with 50 rounds. (The idea had been to develop a version optimised for intercepting high-flying drifting reconnaissance balloons – the stillborn Yak-25PA.)

Prototype construction was completed in early 1959. Coded '75 Yellow', the aircraft entered flight test on 1st March 1959 (about three months later than anticipated) with project test pilot Vladimir P. Smirnov at the controls. Test pilot Aleksey A. Shcherbakov of the Flight Research Institute named after Mikhail M. Gromov (LII – *Lyotno-issle-dovatel'skiy instituut*) also flew the aircraft. The test programme was completed successfully on 29th May 1959. The prototype's empty weight was 6,175 kg (13,613 lb) and

all-up weight was 9,800 kg (21,605 lb). During trials the Yak-25RV attained a maximum altitude of 21,000 m (68,900 ft) and a top speed of Mach 0.82, which was considered adequate for a high-altitude reconnaissance aircraft.

Smirnov reported that the Yak-25RV's handling was broadly similar to other jets at up to 11,000 m (36,090 ft) and climbing to 18,500-19,500 m (60,695-63,980 ft) presented no problems. Above that, however, the pilot had to exercise special care because the Yak-25RV's speed envelope was extremely narrow – the never-exceed speed (V_{NE}) was just 10 km/h (6.2 mph) above the stalling speed because of the rarefied air at high altitude. This put constant pressure on the pilots; as service pilots converting to the Yak-25RV from the Sukhoi Su-9 *Fishpot-B* interceptor put it, 'you have to keep your ears pricked!' Thankfully the aircraft gave ample warning that the limit was near; at minimum control speed it would start swaying from side to side with increasing amplitude, and at V_{NE} it would start vibrating noisily.

The service ceiling could not be determined because the engines tended to flame out at 19,600-20,100 m (64,300-65,940 ft) and there was no oxygen feed system to facilitate restarting, which meant the aircraft had to descend to 6,000 m (19,680 ft) before a restart became possible. The pilot had to wear a special SI-3M pressure suit which also drew some criticism – it was cumbersome like a diver's suit and tended to inflate, hampering the pilot's actions.

A curious feature of the Yak-25RV was its reluctance to descend from high altitude. In one of the test flights, when Smirnov had reached maximum altitude, he discovered that the aircraft was firmly intent on staying up there; only when the landing gear was extended did the prototype start descending slowly. Later, Shcherbakov had a similar experience. In his test report he suggested

that the Yakovlev OKB incorporate some device reducing the aircraft's lift/drag ratio in order to facilitate descent (the Yak-25RV lacked the interceptor's lateral airbrakes). One more peculiarity of the Yak-25RV was its extremely flat glideslope on landing as compared to contemporary jets.

Upon completion of the manufacturer's flight tests the Yak-25RV was prepared for an attempt on the world altitude record. On 13th July 1954 Vladimir P. Smirnov reached 20,456 m (67,112 ft) with a 1,000-kg (2,204-lb) payload; sixteen days later he set a second record by reaching 20,174 m (66,187 ft) with a 2,000-kg (4,409-lb) payload. In the *Fédération Aéronautique Internationale* (FAI) papers acknowledging the records the aircraft type was stated simply as 'RV', which caused some Western analysts to decipher this abbreviation erroneously as re**kord** *vyso***ty** (altitude record) – probably by analogy with the Tupolev ANT-25 record-breaking aircraft of 1930s fame, which was known as RD (re**kord** **dahl'***nosti* – range record). It should be noted here that, reluctant to reveal the true identity of combat aircraft setting various world records, the Soviet aviation authorities would often furnish bogus aircraft and engine designations for the FAI documents. Thus, a specially-modified Sukhoi Su-27P *Flanker-B* interceptor used to set a number of time-to-height and altitude records in 1986-87 was entered as the P-42, while its Lyul'ka AL-31F afterburning turbofans were reported as 'R-32 jet engines'. In the case of the Yak-25RV this, of course, was a coincidence both the FAI and the USSR could live with!

Incidentally, these were not the only records set by the type. On 11th August 1965 test pilot Marina L. Popovich set a female world speed record in a modified Yak-25RV, averaging 753.048 km/h (407.05 kts) over a 2,000-km (1,242-mile) closed circuit. Two years later, on 18th September 1967, she set another official world record,

Opposite, bottom: The second prototype ('76 Yellow') was completed as the Yak-25RV-I target aircraft. This view illustrates the bicycle landing gear with wingtip-mounted outrigger struts and the ventral oil cooler scoops on the engine nacelles. Note also the two extra pitots.

Below: Three-quarters rear view of the Yak-25RV, showing the tracer flares at the base of the rudder (a feature specific to the target version to facilitate night interception). Note the absence of airbrakes – a feature that caused problems for Yak-25RV pilots.

Side view of a production Yak-25RV ('20 Yellow'), showing to advantage the slim fuselage and the shape of the nosecone.

covering a distance of 2,497.009 km (1,550.93 miles) on a closed circuit.

State acceptance trials took place between 5th May and 1st August 1961. Pyotr N. Belyasnik was project test pilot; the Yak-25RV was also flown by Vasiliy G. Ivanov, Nikolay P. Zakharov, Vasiliy S. Kotlov, Pyotr F. Kabrelyov, Gheorgiy T. Beregovoy, Igor' I. Lesnikov and Viktor V. Yatsun. The trials turned up a few deficiencies. Due to the lack of airbrakes the Yak-25RV could fly at 12,000-16,000 m (39,370-52,490 ft) only with the gear down because, even with the engines at flight idle, it was overpowered and could easily exceed V_NE. Also, the lack of a de-icing system and exterior lighting meant the aircraft could operate in daytime visual meteorological conditions only.

The Soviet Air Force was not completely satisfied with the aircraft's performance; still, there was no alternative design. As the Yak-25RV did have a high service ceiling and good endurance (during a test flight on 10th April 1961 LII test pilot Boris V. Polovnikov stayed aloft for 5 hours 30 minutes), the VVS reluctantly gave the go-ahead for series production. After a few detail changes the Yak-25RV passed its State acceptance trials and entered production at the Ulan-Ude aircraft factory No. 99 under the in-house code *izdeliye* (product) 25RV. Production aircraft had two additional pitots flanking the nose-mounted air data boom; additionally, late-production Yak-25RVs had a flat-bottomed dielectric fairing aft of the main gear unit. The Yak-25RV received the NATO reporting name *Mandrake* in the 'miscellaneous' series.

In 1961 there was a curious episode when Belyasnik and Kabrelyov were ferrying the first production Yak-25RVs from Ulan-Ude to the GK NII VVS test facility in Akhtoobinsk. '*We were assigned flight level 12,000 m,* – Belyasnik recalled, – *but the aircraft would not maintain level flight at this altitude and we kept climbing all the while. When we were between Novosibirsk and Sverdlovsk the traffic controller requested our flight level. I replied "Zero sixteen"; I could not state in clear code that we were at 16,000 m. The irate controller ordered us to descend, otherwise he would send PVO fighters after us. I had to answer back impudently, "I don't care if you send the whole damn regiment after us – you won't get us anyway. We are not causing trouble for anyone, and we cannot descend."*

Starting in 1964 a handful of Yak-25RVs was converted for radiation intelligence (RINT) duties associated with nuclear weapons tests. Designated **Yak-25RR** (*radiatsionnyy razvedchik* – RINT aircraft), they had two underwing pylons (strut-braced on the inboard side) for carrying standardised RR8311-100 air sampling pods. Originally developed in 1964 for the Yak-28RR tactical reconnaissance aircraft, these pods had a nose intake closed by a movable cone and a paper filter which arrested dust particles, enabling their radiation level to be measured on the ground. Such pods were also carried by the Antonov An-12RR *Cub*, An-24RR *Coke* and An-30R *Clank* RINT aircraft, one of several Tupolev Tu-16R reconnaissance versions (*Badger-F*) and occasionally the Tu-95K-22 *Bear-G* naval missile strike aircraft. The drag generated by the pods impaired the aircraft's performance, reducing the service ceiling to 17,000 m (55,780 ft).

On 9th-26th October 1971 a modified Yak-25RR (c/n 25991201) underwent tests at the Yakovlev OKB's flight test facility in

Zhukovskiy. Designated **Yak-25RRV** (*rah-diotekh****nich****eskiy razvedchik, vysotnyy* – electronic intelligence aircraft, high-altitude), the aircraft was developed pursuant to ruling No. 111 issued by the Council of Ministers Presidium' Commission on Defence Matters dated 7th May 1968 to suit a Ministry of Defence requirement. The Yak-25RRV was based on the Yak-25RR. The air sampling pods were replaced with special pods housing a signals intelligence (SIGINT) system designated IRIS (*izme****rit****el'-reghi****strah****tor* ***im****pool's-nykh si****gnah****lov* – [electromagnetic] pulse signal measurement and recording device), aka *Vol****na****-S* (Wave-S); it was designed to detect and record electromagnetic pulses emitted by radars and the like. The cylindrical pods had parabolic dielectric fairings at both ends, with two probe aerials pointing forward and upward at the front; they were pressurised and heated by engine bleed air to make sure the equipment would operate normally at high altitude. The cockpit featured a new control panel for the SIGINT suite; some minor changes were made to other systems. Tests showed that the new pods and the associated air ducts had virtually no negative effect on the aircraft's performance. The Yak-25RRV was built in very small numbers (the exact quantity is unknown).

For the sake of completeness we may add that the *Mandrake* had a couple of other versions not associated with reconnaissance. These were the Yak-25RV-I manned target aircraft emulating high-flying spyplanes for the benefit of Air Defence Force fighter pilots (this did *not* involve live firing – only the gun camera would be used to record a 'kill') and the Yak-25RV-II remote-controlled target drone for live weapons training. Between 1961 and 1965 a total of 155 *Mandrakes* was built, of which less than half were regular Yak-25RV, Yak-25RR and Yak-25RRV spyplanes.

YAK-25RV IN SERVICE

The Yak-25RV stayed in service for about fifteen years until superseded by the Mikoyan MiG-25R and subsequent versions (see below). Performance-wise it was broadly similar to the U-2R, with the exception of range. Its safety record was quite good, no aircraft being lost in accidents. Apart from the southern and western areas of the Soviet Union, the *Mandrake* was deployed with the Group of Soviet Forces in Germany: an unidentified unit based at Zerbst in (former) East Germany operated three Yak-25RVs from 1966 until the early 1970s. In July 1966 these aircraft were used for target practice (probably for the Northern Group of Forces, i.e., Soviet forces in Poland), flying over Poland at 19,000 m (62,340 ft) and emulating Western intruders. Makes you wonder if this was also a photography practice mission for the *Mandrake* pilots! In 1962-63 the 14th *Leningradskiy* Red Banner GvIAP (*Gvar****dey****skiy istre****bit****el'nyy* ***avia****polk* – Guards Fighter Regiment) of the Southern Group of Forces, which was stationed at Kiskunlacháza, Hungary, operated two to four Yak-25RVs alongside its Mikoyan MiG-21PF *Fishbed-D* interceptors.

Oddly enough, despite being stationed in East Germany and Hungary the Yak-25RV was never noted over Western Europe (either due to extremely limited numbers or thanks to careful mission planning); at least, Western sources do not mention any sightings. On the other hand, it *was* noted over China, India and Pakistan. When the type was phased out in the early 1970s, surviving aircraft were either converted to Yak-25RV-II drones and shot down or simply scrapped. Fortunately, a single example survives at the Central Russian Air Force Museum in Monino near Moscow.

A flight of operational Yak-25RV-I; except for the tracer, they are outwardly identical to the 'pure' reconnaissance version. Unfortunately, as photography at Soviet airbases was expressly forbidden in the 1950s and 1960s, no high-quality photos of operational Yak-25RVs have surfaced to date.

THE *MANDRAKE* IN DETAIL

The following brief structural description applies to the production Yak-25RV.

The fuselage of basically circular cross-section changing to elliptical at the rear is a riveted semi-monocoque stressed-skin duralumin structure with 48 frames and 38 stringers; maximum diameter is 1.45 m (4 ft 9⁵⁄₆₄ in.). The forward fuselage incorporates an avionics/equipment bay (frames 0-5) accessible via dorsal and lateral hatches; a metal nosecone carrying a PVD-7 pitot is attached to frame 0. The single-seat cockpit (frames 5-11) is enclosed by a sliding canopy with a fixed windshield incorporating an optically flat windscreen which is electrically de-iced. The canopy blends into a shallow spine housing control runs, piping and electric wiring. The nosewheel well is located between frames 4-9. The cockpit is pressurised and air-conditioned by engine bleed air which is cooled in a cooling turbine. The centre fuselage accommodates the fuel tanks and the mainwheel well (frames 19-23). The rear fuselage incorporates a camera bay with ventral doors between frames 31-33; it terminates in a metal tailcone attached to frame 44.

The cantilever mid-set wings of trapezoidal planform have no sweepback at quarter-chord. They are all-metal stressed-skin two-spar structures, the spars passing through the fuselage at frames 21 and 24. Each wing has 38 ribs and is built in two sections joined at rib 18. The outer wings terminate in tip fairings housing the landing gear outrigger struts. The wings have no high-lift devices and are fitted with two-section ailerons.

The sweptback cantilever cruciform tail surfaces are of all-metal stressed-skin construction. The *vertical tail* comprises a two-spar fin attached to rear fuselage frames 34 and 37, with a large root fillet, and a two-piece rudder. The *horizontal tail* comprises stabilisers and one-piece elevators; stabiliser incidence is adjusted by a hydraulic motor.

The pneumatically-retractable bicycle landing gear comprises a steerable nose unit with a single 600 x 155 mm (23.62 x 6.10 in) wheel, a main unit with twin 800 x 225 mm (31.49 x 8.85 in) wheels and outrigger struts with single 310 x 135 mm (12.24 x 5.31 in) wheels at the wingtips. The nose and main units retract aft, the outrigger struts forward. All units have oleo-pneumatic shock absorbers; the mainwheels have pneumatic brakes.

The Yak-25RV is powered by two Tumanskiy R11V-300 axial-flow non-afterburning turbojets rated at 4,000 kgp (8,820 lbst) for

Four views of the Yak-25RV in the open-air display of the Central Russian Air Force Museum in Monino. Note the camera window fairing, seen in the three-quarter rear view, under the rear fuselage, with the radio altimeter dipole aerials fore and aft of it, and the absence of trailing-edge flaps on the wings.

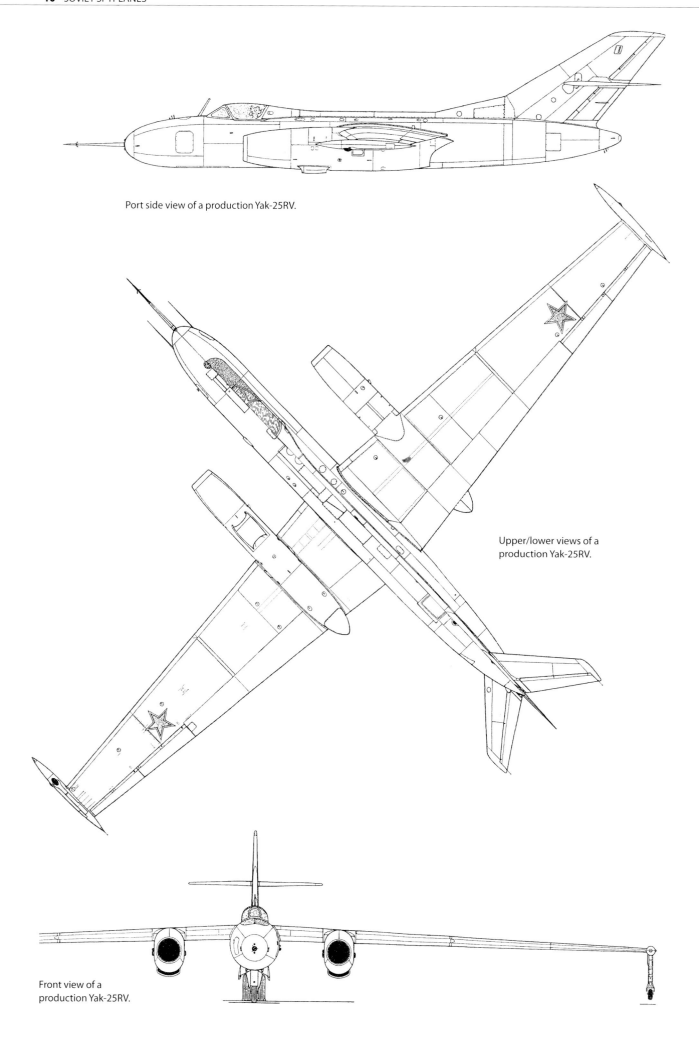

Port side view of a production Yak-25RV.

Upper/lower views of a production Yak-25RV.

Front view of a production Yak-25RV.

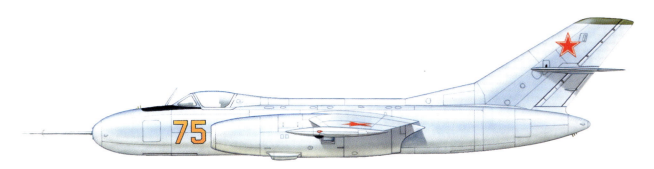

take-off and 3,250 kgp (7,165 lbst) at nominal power. The R11V-300 has a six-stage axial compressor, a can-annular combustion chamber, a two-stage turbine and a fixed-area nozzle. Starting is electric. The engines are housed in streamlined nacelles attached to the wing underside between ribs 6-9. The nacelles have detachable inlet sections and ventral oil cooler housings.

The aircraft has conventional mechanical flight controls with push-pull rods, bell-cranks and levers. The aileron control circuit incorporates a centrally located BU-8Yu irreversible hydraulic actuator.

All fuel is housed in three bladder tanks in the centre fuselage. Each tank has its own PN-45I pump. There is also a small tank holding petrol to facilitate engine starting/relight.

Hydraulic power is used for the aileron actuator, nosewheel steering and stabiliser trim mechanism. The hydraulic system is powered by an NP-24 pump driven by the starboard engine's accessory gearbox. Main DC power is provided by the engines' GSR-ST-12000VT starter-generators, with a DC battery as a back-up. AC power for the equipment is provided by PO-500 single-phase AC converters and a PT-70Ts three-phase AC converter. There are two pneumatic systems used for landing gear, flap, wheel brake and camera bay door operation, as well as for sealing the canopy.

The avionics suite includes an OSP-48 *Materik* (Continent) instrument landing system (with an ARK-9 automatic direction finder), an RSIU-5 UHF communications radio, an SRO-2M *Khrom-Nikel'* (Chromium-Nickel; NATO *Odd Rods*) identification friend-or-foe (IFF) transponder etc. Mission equipment comprises an AFA-40 vertical camera (*aerofotoapparaht* – aerial camera) mounted in a rear fuselage bay.

The pilot is equipped with an SI-3M pressure suit for high-altitude operations; a supply of liquid oxygen (LOX) and a LOX converter are provided. The pilot sits on a pneumatically operated ejection seat.

The first prototype Yak-25RV which is depicted on the box top of the Amodel Yak-25RV-II kit. The aircraft had a natural metal finish.

■ YAK-25RV BASIC DATA

Length	15.93 m (52 ft 3½ in)
Wing span	23.4 m (76 ft 9¼ in)
Height on ground	4.3 m (14 ft 1¹¹⁄₆₄ in)
Wing area, m² (sq ft)	55.0 (591.39)
Empty weight, kg (lb)	6,175 (13,610)
Take-off weight, kg (lb)	9,800 (21,600)
Speed, km/h (mph):	
at sea level	500 (310)
at high altitude	870 (540) or Mach 0.82
Range, km (miles)	3,500 (2,174)
Service ceiling, m (ft)	20,500 (67,260)

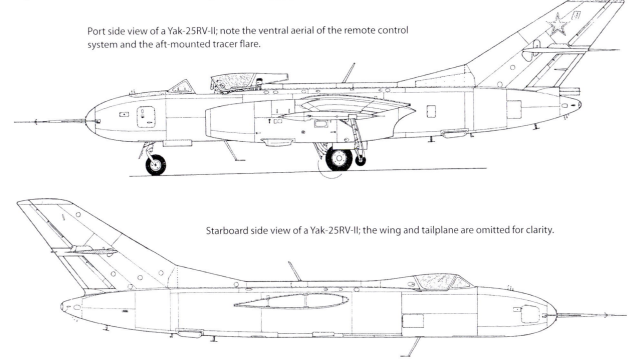

Port side view of a Yak-25RV-II; note the ventral aerial of the remote control system and the aft-mounted tracer flare.

Starboard side view of a Yak-25RV-II; the wing and tailplane are omitted for clarity.

The Modeller's Corner

Due to its classified nature and the small number of aircraft built the Yak-25RV has been neglected by the model kit manufacturers until the 2000s. So far there are only four kits (with variations) of the *Mandrake* on the market.

BROPLAN **YAK-25RV**   1:72nd scale

The first kit of the type on the market was a vacuform kit by the Polish company BroPlan.

The model is still available, though quite rare, but its accuracy is open to question.

The BroPlan Yak-25RV vacuform model built by Jim Lund.

PROP & JET **YAK-25RV**   1:72nd scale

Another vacuform kit was released in 2004 by Prop & Jet – a one-man operation by Musa Zakoreyev based in Nal'chik, Russia, which specialises in little-known aircraft types. The model (Ref. No. 7221) is based on the scale plans that accompanied a monograph on the Yak-25RV in the Ukrainian magazine *Aviatsiya i Vremya* (No. 6-1997).

The kit features two sheets of 0.5-mm

The Prop & Jet Yak-25RV kit box art showing the aircraft in the Monino museum.

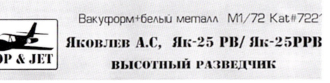

white polystyrene with a total of 48 parts, and a clear acrylic sheet with the canopy (which requires Superglue). The basic airframe components feature engraved panel lines, and even the various small air scoops are faithfully reproduced. Curiously, the sheets feature an IRIS ELINT pod – but only one, so if you fancy a Yak-25RRV you'd have to build the other pod from scratch. The landing gear struts, pitot boom, radio aerial, control stick and rudder pedals are cast in white metal, with a bit of flash here and there that requires careful removal; the wingtip outrigger struts are cast together with the wheels, and the main gear retraction jack is a separate item. The ejection seat is cast in polyester resin.

The kit comes with an A4 format instruction sheet (featuring a summary of the aircraft's development history) and a small decal sheet by the Russian manufacturer Begemot featuring eight Soviet stars (in two sizes) and two tactical codes ('01 Yellow' and '03 Red') but no decal for the instrument panel, which is included. Today, the Prop & Jet kit is no longer in production and has become a rarity.

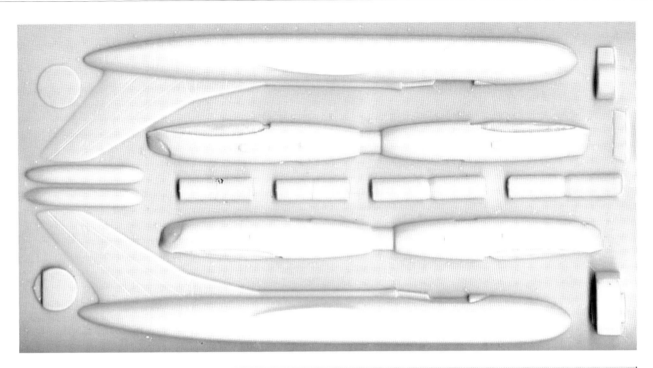

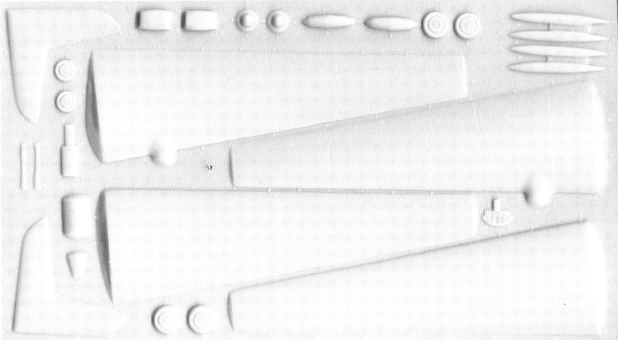

Above: The plastic sheets with the principal airframe parts. Note that parts for only one IRIS pod are included.

Below left: The ejection seat is cast in resin. **Right:** The cockpit canopy.

Below right: The white metal parts – the landing gear struts, stick, rudder pedals, nose probe and blade aerial. Note that the main gear retraction jack comes as a separate part.

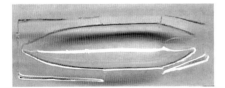

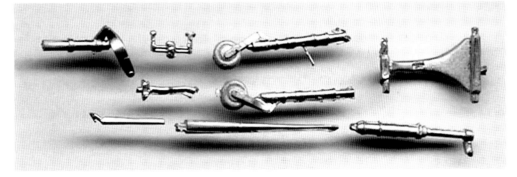

Three views of a completed Prop & Jet Yak-25RV built by Yevgeniy Dedigoorov. The outsize canopy is a replacement part that had to be manufactured because the original one was scratched, and the modeller made an error in making the canopy. Apart from that, the correct choice of background, lighting and aspect work wonders – the model looks almost like the real thing.

AMODEL **YAK-25RV/-25RRV/-25RV-II**   1:72nd scale

The third 1:72nd scale offering is by the Ukrainian manufacturer Amodel, which has made a name for itself by catering for modellers who want something outside the mainstream. In fact, Amodel offers two different versions of the *Mandrake*, using the injection moulded/'short run' technology.

The first kit (Ref. No. 72176) released in 2011 represents the baseline Yak-25RV, with an option to build the Yak-25RRV ELINT version. The box contains eight sprues moulded in dark grey or brown plastic plus one clear sprue (82 parts in all); the 12 parts for the IRIS pods are conveniently located on a separate sprue. Again, the model fits quite well into the abovementioned scale plans. The moulding quality is passable, with no flash and engraved panel lines; the latter, however, are vague at times. Also, modellers report that the parts do not fit together too well, requiring quite a bit of putty here and there.

The kit comes with clear Russian/English instructions and a small decal sheet of rather poor quality that allows you to build either of the two prototype ('75 Yellow' or '76 Yellow'). The box art, however, shows a Yak-25RRV wearing no tactical code. The finished model is 225 mm long, with a span of 334 mm.

The other kit (Ref. No. 72212) represents the Yak-25RV-II and consists of 64 parts; it lacks the ELINT pods but features parts unique to the target drone (remote control aerials, tracer flare holders etc.). The stock decal sheet is for an aircraft coded '76 Yellow', but there is also a limited edition (Ref. No. 72212-01) released in 500 copies with different decals and painting instructions to build a silver/red example serialled '984 Red'.

Above: The box art of the Amodel Yak-25RV/Yak-25RRV kit shows the RRV version.

Below: Confusingly, the box top of the Amodel Yak-25RV-II kit with stock decals shows the Yak-25RV prototype, not the target drone version.

Bottom: The Yak-25RV-II kit is available as a limited edition (of 500) with different decals as denoted by the additional Sova ('Owl') logo.

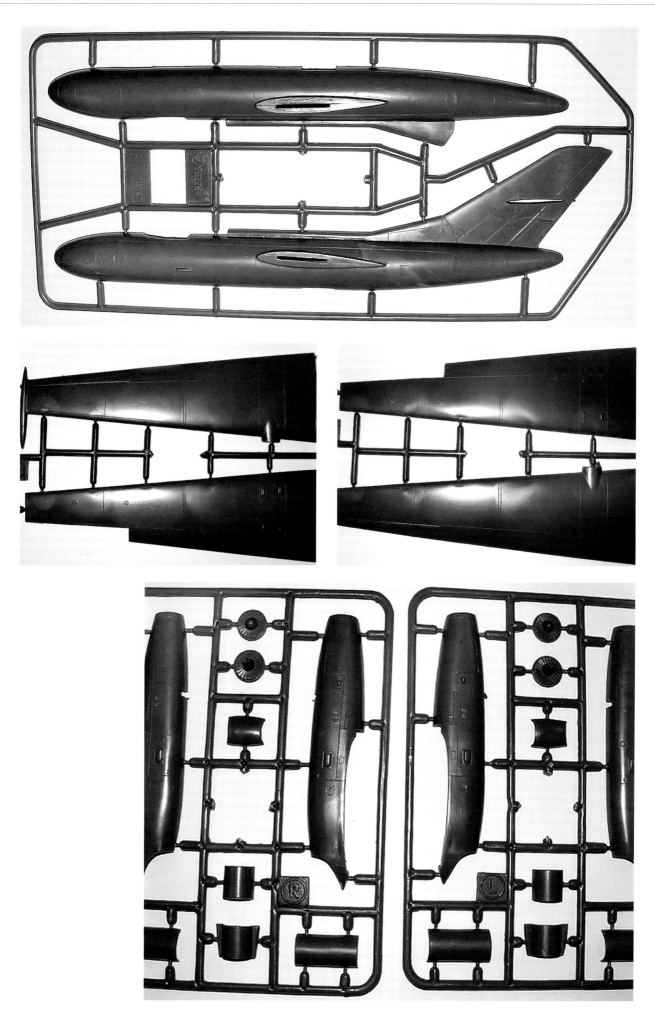

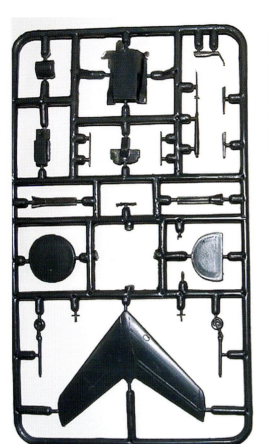
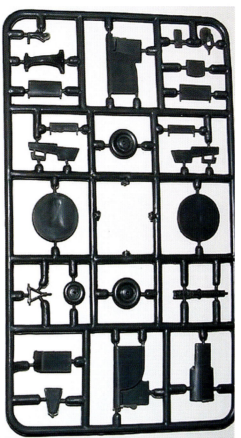

Opposite and above:
The basic components of the Yak-25RV kit.

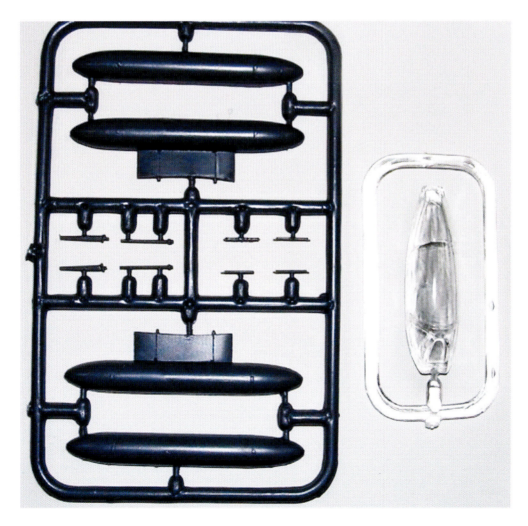

Left: The clear sprue includes only the canopy, which is fairly thick. The parts for the optional IRIS ELINT pods (including aerials and sway braces) come as a separate sprue.

The Amodel Yak-25RV built by Vadim Lysenko. The stock canopy has been replaced by a thinner two-piece version and is opened to show the cockpit interior. The modeller used Mr. Color paints, plus Tamiya paints for weathering.

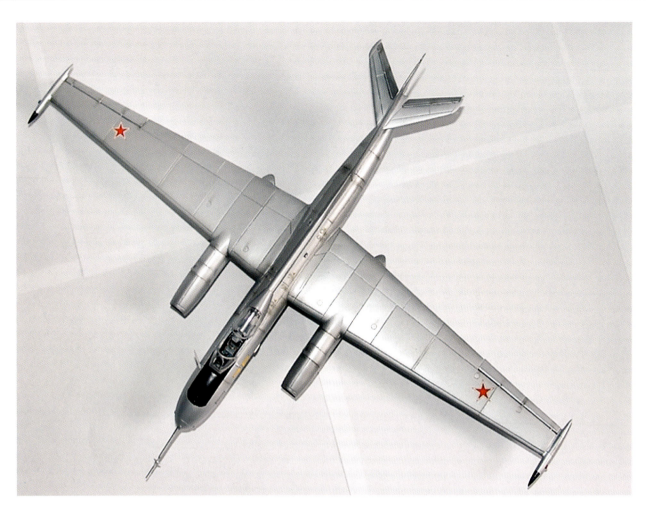

Opposite page: Upper and lower views of the model.

This page: Lower views of the model.

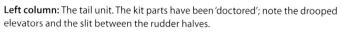

Left column: The tail unit. The kit parts have been 'doctored'; note the drooped elevators and the slit between the rudder halves.

Right column and opposte page: Detail views of the landing gear, with additional parts made of stretched sprue.

Below left: Detail of the nose, with modified pitot and added landing light.

Below: The port wingtip and aileron; note the added navigation light.

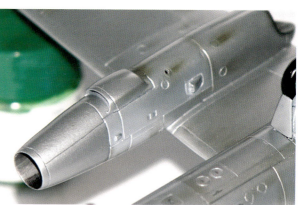

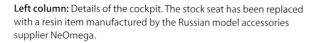

Left column: Details of the cockpit. The stock seat has been replaced with a resin item manufactured by the Russian model accessories supplier NeOmega.

Right column: Details of the engine nacelles. The inlets and exhausts have also been modified for added realism.

ANIGRAND CRAFTSWORK **YAK-25RV**   1:144th scale

The fourth model is to 1:144th scale (definitely too small to do the aircraft justice) and is offered by the Chinese manufacturer Anigrand Craftswork. It is not a stand-alone kit, coming as a bonus to the 1:144th scale Bartini 14M1P kit (Ref. No. AA-4044). The model is cast in polyester resin and consists of just 16 parts, including a clear plastic canopy. No decals are included; thank goodness that at least the landing gear is there.

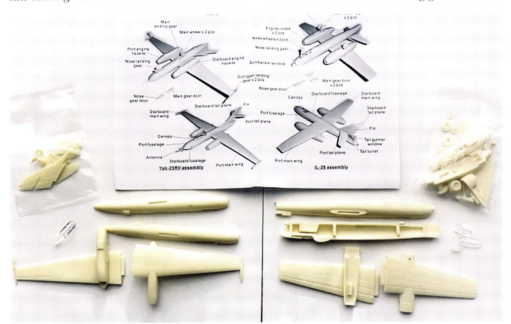

The Anigrand Yak-25RV, together with another bonus model from the same kit – the IL-28. Note how the engine nacelles are manufactured together with the wings as one-piece castings, despite being listed in the instruction sheet as separate parts.

The Anigrand Yak-25RV built by Thomas Peters.

Further views of the
Anigrand Yak-25RV
built by Thomas Peters.

Mach 2.5 Spy

The Mikoyan MiG-25R Series

When the US Air Force introduced the Convair B-58 Hustler supersonic bomber and the Lockheed SR-71 Blackbird Mach 3 reconnaissance aircraft programme got under way, the Soviet government was compelled to give an adequate answer to these threats. Hence the design bureau led by Artyom I. Mikoyan and Mikhail I. Gurevich (OKB-155) was tasked with developing a new supersonic heavy interceptor.

Preliminary design (PD) work started as early as 1958, the aircraft being allocated the designation Ye-155. (The Ye prefix stood for *yedinitsa* – 'unit', or perhaps 'one-off' aircraft; it was used to designate Mikoyan prototypes up to and including the MiG-31.) However, development did not begin in earnest until mid-1959. The project aroused the interest of the Soviet Air Defence Force (PVO) command, which needed a high-speed high-altitude interceptor, and the Soviet Air Force (VVS – *Voyenno-vozdooshnyye seely*), which wanted a new reconnaissance platform. Since the operational requirements set forth by the PVO and the VVS for these aircraft were broadly similar (a top speed of around Mach 3 and a service ceiling in excess of 20,000 m/65,620 ft), it was decided to design a joint-service aircraft to fill both roles. A Council of Ministers/Communist Party Central Committee directive issued In February 1961 tasked the Mikoyan OKB with developing the Ye-155P interceptor (*perekhvatchik*) and Ye-155R reconnaissance aircraft (*razvedchik*). On 10th March 1961, Artyom I. Mikoyan formally launched the design work.

The configuration selected eventually was a shoulder-wing aircraft with moderately swept trapezoidal wings, twin tails and two engines located side by side in the rear fuselage, with lateral two-dimensional air intakes. The only suitable engine was the huge R15B-300 axial-flow afterburning turbojet designed by Aleksandr A. Mikulin and his closest aide Sergey K. Tumanskiy at OKB-300. The airframe was largely made of high-strength stainless steel accounting for up to 80% of the structural weight. The choice of steel as the principal structural material turned out to be correct. The Soviet designers proved unable to overcome the cracking problem affecting thin-walled welded titanium structures, not to mention the fact that steel was a lot cheaper. Highly efficient cooling systems and heat insulation technologies were devised to overcome the strong kinetic heating that would occur at the Ye-155's operational speeds. For the same reason a special T-6 grade jet fuel with a high flash point was used to reduce the danger of explosion.

The Ye-155R was to be equipped with the all-new *Peleng* (Bearing) long-range radio navigation system with course correction from an inertial navigation system (INS). LII and the All-Union Electronics and Automatic Equipment Research Institute (VNIIRA – *Vsesoyooznyy naoochno-issledovatel'skiy instItoot rahdioelektroniki i avtomahtiki*) initiated the development of the *Polyot* (Flight) flight/navigation suite that would allow the Ye-155 to follow a planned course, then return to base and make an automatic approach; it also provided inputs to mission equipment.

Eight interchangeable reconnaissance suites were proposed. Version 1 was intended for photo reconnaissance (PHOTINT) and SIGINT. The mission equipment comprised five cameras – three AFA-44s (two oblique and one vertical) and two AFA-42s – and an SRS-4A SIGINT pack (*stahntsiya razvedki svyazi*). Version 2 was fitted with four AFA-45 cameras, one AFA-44 and two AFA-42s, plus the SRS-4A SIGINT pack. Version 3 carried an AShchAFA-5 or AShchAFA-6 slot camera (*avtomaticheskiy shchelevoy aerofotoapparaht*) for continuous shooting, plus one AFA-44 and two AFA-42s. A Bariy-1 (Barium) television system could also be fitted. Version 4 carried an AFA-41 camera on a TAU mount (*topograficheskaya aerofotoustanovka* topographic aerial camera mount), one AFA-44, two AFA-42s and the Bariy-1 TV system. Version 5 was configured for night PHOTINT with two NAFA-MK or NAFA-100 night cameras (*nochnoy aerofotoapparaht*). It carried 12 FotAB-100 flare bombs (*fotograficheskaya aviabomba*) or 60 FotAB-MG flares and could also be fitted with the SRS-4A pack. Version 6 carried a NAFA-Ya-7 camera coupled with a *Yavor*-7 (Sycamore) airborne flash unit and the SRS-4A pack. Version 7 was to carry thermal imaging equipment. Finally, version 8 was tailored for ELINT, with SRS-4A/SRS-4B and Romb-3 (Rhombus, or Diamond) general-purpose SIGINT packs and a Koob-3 (Cube) suite for detailed SIGINT. The SRS-4A could detect centimetre- and decimetre-waveband radars; its aerials were located on the forward fuselage sides behind dielectric panels. After being picked up, the radar signal was amplified, classed by frequency, converted and

Above: '1155 Red', the first prototype MiG-25R (Ye-155R-1), at Zhukovskiy during tests. Note the small vertical tails, the large ventral fins, the wingtip tanks with large 'inverted winglets', the shape of the dielectric panel on the nose and the (as-yet non-functional) camera port; all of these features would change on the production version. Note also the star insignia on the fuselage.

Below: '3155 Red', the third prototype (Ye-155R-3), with the huge 5,300-litre drop tank in place. The tip tanks have already given place to anti-flutter weights. The aircraft carried a full camera fit (note the functional camera port). The fairings on the air intake trunks enclose fittings for the envisaged canard foreplanes, which never materialised.

recorded on film by a special camera. The SRS-4B differed only in the range of detectable frequencies.

The VVS dismissed this as inefficient and came up with new requirements in March 1961. The range of targets and the equipment suite were specified more clearly, more stringent requirements applying. Small targets such as bridges had to be pinpointed with a 100-150-m (330-500-ft) error margin; for large-area targets the error margin was 300-400 m (990-1,300 ft). Intelligence was to be transferred via data link within three to five minutes after passing over the target. The navigation suite was to operate with an error margin of 0.8-1% in areas devoid of landmarks, ensuring a target approach accuracy of ±200-300 m (660-990 ft).

The PHOTINT/ELINT version was to carry an SRS-4A or SRS-4B SIGINT pack and seven interchangeable camera sets intended for (a) high-altitude general daylight recce, (b) high-altitude detailed daylight recce, (c) low-level day recce, (d) topographic daylight recce, (e) high-altitude night recce, (f) medium-altitude night recce and (g) low-level night recce. The detailed ELINT version was fitted with a Koob-3 SIGINT suite and a *Voskhod* (Sunrise) metre-waveband side-looking airborne radar (SLAR). Finally, the third version had an *Igla* (Needle) SLAR and a TV system.

This proposal was accepted, albeit with major revisions. The designers did some homework and pointed out that the chances of penetrating the enemy air defences at medium altitude would be virtually nil. Hence the principal reconnaissance mode would be high-altitude supersonic flight; this, in turn, necessitated an increase in the cameras' focal lengths. In the early 1960s the Krasnogorsk Optics and Machinery Plant brought out a hitherto unseen piece of hardware – the AFA-70 four-lens aerial camera.

Designated Ye-155R-1, the first prototype took a full year to complete and was rolled out the Mikoyan OKB's prototype construction facility in December 1963. It made its first flight on 6th March, flown by OKB-155's chief test pilot Aleksandr V. Fedotov. In 1965 the second prototype (Ye-155R-2) joined the trials, allowing the scope of the programme to be expanded appreciably. Meanwhile, aircraft factory No. 21 in Gor'kiy (now Nizhniy Novgorod) was tooling up for production, the reconnaissance version receiving the in-house product code *izdeliye* 02. The third prototype, Ye-155R-3, was the first Gor'kiy-built pre-production example; rolled out on 6th May 1966, it carried a complete camera fit and avionics suite and had various structural changes Joint State acceptance trials performed jointly by OKB-155 and the Air Force were carried out chiefly by GNIKI VVS in Akhtoobinsk, Astrakhan' Region, in southern Russia. Col. Aleksandr S. Bezhevets was project test pilot; the Ye-155R-3 was also flown by Mikoyan OKB test pilots Aleksandr V. Fedotov, Pyotr M. Ostapenko, Boris A. Orlov, Oleg V. Goodkov, A. A. Kravtsov, Igor' I. Lesnikov and others.

A comprehensive research programme was held to find out how the Ye-155R's flight modes would affect the performance of the reconnaissance cameras. Fortunately, the tests showed there was no reason to worry about picture quality. At an altitude of 20,000 m (65,620 ft) the A-72 and A-70M cameras had a resolution of 30 cm (11¾ in) and 40 cm (15¾ in) respectively; This made it possible to make out objects measuring 1.5 x 1.5 m (4 ft 11 in x 4 ft 11 in) for the A-72 or 2-2.5 x 2-2.5 m (6 ft 6 in to 8 ft 2 in x 6 ft 6 in to 8 ft 2 in) for the A-70M, or even smaller objects if the contrast quotient was higher.

Coded '024 Red' (that is, *izdeliye* 02, airframe No. 4), the Ye-155R-4 represented the production standard configuration, featuring a number of changes. Firstly, the fins were significantly enlarged and recontoured, featuring a slight leading edge kink at the roots and reduced trailing-edge sweep; conversely, the ventral fins were downsized, which reduced the risk of a tailstrike. The slab stabilisers (stabilators), which until then had been used only for pitch control, could now be deflected differentially to assist roll control. Wing anhedral was increased to 5°. Secondly, the extreme nose had an ogival shape instead of double curvature and featured a dielectric tip; the lateral dielectric panels were reshaped and repositioned. The aircraft served for performance testing and reconnaissance suite calibration. Several new items were also tested on this machine, namely the Peleng-S and Polyot-1I navigation systems, several interchangeable liquid-cooled pallet-mounted ECM sets and the Prizma HF radio set.

IN PRODUCTION

The test programme lasted several years, during which the prototypes made several hundred flights. Finally, in 1967 the State Commission cleared the reconnaissance version for production, the Ye-155R receiving the service designation **MiG-25R**. The first production MiG-25Rs started rolling off the production line in 1969. The deficiencies noted in the course of the State acceptance trials and the service introduction period were quickly remedied. As the Gor'kiy factory reequipped with more up-to-date tooling, production became less labour-intensive and costly, and the MiG-25R's production rate started to grow.

The equipment suite of the production MiG-25R comprised four A-70M oblique cameras for general-purpose PHOTINT and one A/E-10 topographic camera with a 1,300-mm focal length. These cameras were developed by the 'Zenit' Optics and Machinery Plant in Krasnogorsk (KOMZ – *Krasnogorskiy optiko-mekhanicheskiy zavod*) under A. Beshenov and enabled pictures to be taken at flight levels of up to 22,000 m (72,180 ft). The cameras fired through five optically flat windows in the underside of the nose.

Unlike the interceptor, the reconnaissance version had integral fuel tanks in the fins to extend range. For self-protection the MiG-25R featured a Siren' (Lilac, pronounced *see**ren'***) active jammer; any of three versions – the SPS-141 Siren'-1F (*izdeliye* 141), SPS-142 Siren'-2F (*izdeliye* 142) or SPS-143 Siren'-3F (*izdeliye* 143) – could be fitted. Early aircraft had the KM-1 ejection seat designed in house, which was later replaced by the improved KM-1M. The Peleng-D navigation system was introduced in production from c/n 020 SO 01 (fuselage number 0301).

The first few production aircraft were delivered to the Air Force's 4th TsBP i PLS (*Tsentr boye**voy** podgo**tov**ki i pere-**oo**chivaniya **lyot**novo sos**tah**va* – Combat Training & Aircrew Conversion Centre) in Lipetsk for evolving operational procedures and tactics. The majority, however, went to the Moscow Military District – specifically, to the 47th GvORAP (*Gvar**dey**skiy ot**del'**nyy raz**ved**yvatel'nyy **avia**polk* – Guards Independent Reconnaissance Air Regiment) at Shatalovo AB near Smolensk. This unit, which began operating the type in June–July 1969, was tasked with the operational evaluation programme.

As MiG-25Rs were delivered to the independent (that is, direct reporting) reconnaissance regiments of the VVS Air Armies, each unit initially operated a mixed bag of types. One squadron in the regiment was equipped with MiG-25Rs used for high-altitude day reconnaissance; the other flew obsolescent Yak-27R *Mangrove* tactical reconnaissance jets used chiefly for night and low-level day missions. For evaluation purposes the num-

ber of MiGs per regiment was temporarily increased to 17.

Pilot training proved to be a problem in the absence of a two-seat version. Mikoyan OKB, Gor'kiy factory and VVS test pilots provided assistance to the first-line units, speeding up conversion. However, the problem of staffing the units with computer technicians qualified to work with the MiG-25R was even worse. Hasty changes had to be made to the educational programme at the Air Force Engineering Academy named after Nikolay Ye. Zhukovskiy. Despite these difficulties, the service tests were completed successfully and the MiG-25R became one of the Soviet Air Force's principal reconnaissance aircraft. The NATO reporting name was *Foxbat-B*.

After defeating the Arab states in the Six-Day War of 1967, Israel continued systematically bombing Egyptian military bases and industrial centres. The Egyptian government approached the USSR, requesting technical and military assistance. Supporting Egypt and Syria was politically important for the Soviet Union at the time, since the Arab states were perpetually at war with Israel, which was backed by the USA. The Soviet military leaders, notably Defence Minister Marshal Dmitriy F. Ustinov, decided to use the MiG-25 in the Middle East in the reconnaissance and strike roles (since the MiG-25R could carry flare bombs for night reconnaissance, theoretically there was no reason why it could not carry general-purpose bombs). Test pilot Stepan A. Mikoyan gives a slightly different story: it was Minister of Aircraft Industry Pyotr V. Dement'yev who, inspired by the navigation suite's high accuracy, came up with the idea of using the MiG-25 as a high-altitude bomber. Thus, in late 1969 the Mikoyan OKB was tasked with developing a dual-role

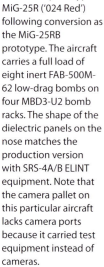

The fourth prototype MiG-25R ('024 Red') following conversion as the MiG-25RB prototype. The aircraft carries a full load of eight inert FAB-500M-62 low-drag bombs on four MBD3-U2 bomb racks. The shape of the dielectric panels on the nose matches the production version with SRS-4A/B ELINT equipment. Note that the camera pallet on this particular aircraft lacks camera ports because it carried test equipment instead of cameras.

A MiG-25R cruises in the stratosphere; the absence of anti-flutter weights identifies it as a very early production.

The same MiG-25R ('45 Blue') shows off the definitive version of the tail unit, with greatly increased vertical tails but smaller ventral fins.

version within three or four weeks; this became known as the **MiG-25RB** (*razvedchik-bombardirovshchik* – recce/strike aircraft), or *izdeliye* 02B.

The changes included the addition of the SUSAB bomb release control system (*sistema oopravleniya sbrosom aviabomb*). To achieve the required bombing accuracy the inputs from the RSBN-6 SHORAN were fed into the modified navigation system designated Peleng-DR. Since the aircraft had no bomb sight (a unique case among bombers!), bomb release was triggered automatically by the navigation computer as the aircraft approached the target with preset coordinates; hence bomb travel calculation software was developed for the navigation computer. A bomb release system was fitted; the bomb shackles were made heat-resistant, safe bomb temperatures were calculated, drop modes devised, and multiple ejector racks (MERs) designed and manufactured. Meanwhile, a special work group was formed to assess the aircraft's chances of survival in the bomber role.

As early as February 1970 the Ye-155R-4 ('024 Red') was converted into the MiG-25RB prototype. In March 1970 Mikoyan OKB test pilot Aviard G. Fastovets made the first bomb drop at 20,000 m (65,620 ft) and 2,500 km/h (1,552 mph) in this aircraft – a world's first, in fact. Later, Air Force test pilots Aleksandr S. Bezhevets and Nikolay I. Stogov took over the main part of the flight testing.

Various defects cropped up during the test programme, ranging from primitive mistakes like electric connectors attached with wrong-grade solder (which melted in high-speed flight due to kinetic heating) to serious problems, such as 'lapses' in the navigation system when following ground beacons in high-altitude flight. The area where the MERs were located under the wings proved hotter than anticipated. On one occasion in April 1970 Bezhevets switched to an alternate test mission involving prolonged supersonic flight; the pyrotechnic cartridges in the MERs overheated and exploded, causing a spontaneous bomb release. To prevent such incidents the racks were moved to a colder

Air Marshal Pavel S. Kutakhov (centre) inspects the 47th GvORAP at Shatalovo AB, with MiG-25RB '49 Blue' in the background. The camera pallet has been lowered to reveal the massive A-70 camera for inspection, resting on its ground handling dolly.

area under the fuselage; this meant only four bombs could be carried, limiting the bomb load to 2,000 km (4,410 lb). New cartridges with a higher blast point were developed later and the designers added the wing pylons again, doubling the bomb load. Tests showed that the specially developed FAB-500M-62T heat-insulated 500-kg (1,102-lb) low-drag HE bombs and the new cartridges could be used throughout the aircraft's speed range. Other types of bombs, including heavier ones, could also be carried.

Bombing accuracy was initially disappointing. The reason was that at altitudes around 23,000 m (75,460 ft) and speeds around 2,500 km/h (1,552 mph) the aircraft would yaw slightly and imperceptibly for the pilot, obeying the autopilot's commands. Even though the bombs would be released at the right moment, even a slight deviation from the intended flight path would cause major aiming errors. It took a lot of effort to cure this defect; as a result, the error margin was reduced to 1 km (0.62 miles) – that is,

Two diagrams showing the strip of land covered by the MiG-25RB's A-70 camera.

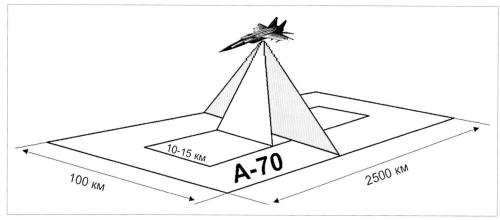

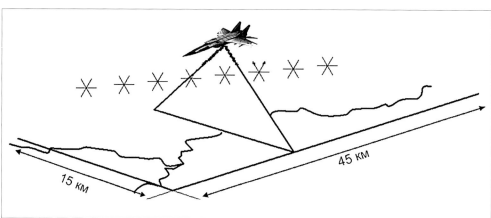

the bomb would drop anywhere within a 2 x 2 km (1.24 x 1.24 mile) square. This was acceptable for nuclear bombs but no good for conventional ones.

When the aircraft was bombed-up the service ceiling decreased slightly. To compensate for this, the area of the air intakes' upper surface was increased. As a result, with a full bomb load, the aircraft's service ceiling was increased by 500-700 m (1,640-2,300 ft) without impairing speed and range.

After that, several production MiG-25Rs were urgently modified to the same standard for service tests in which regular VVS pilots would participate along with test pilots. To increase bombing accuracy, a new Peleng-DM navigation suite was developed, featuring a more accurate INS with float gyros (the old one had special ball bearings), a vertical accelerometer for registering the aircraft's vertical speed at the bomb release point and making corrections, and a correction system receiving inputs from a LORAN system. Additionally, the MiG-25RB and subsequent reconnaissance/strike versions had a Polyot-1I navigation suite comprising the Romb-1K SHORAN/approach system, an attitude & heading reference system (AHRS) and an air data system.

Quite a few bugs had to be eliminated, as it turned out. The navigation computer and INS failed at regular intervals. There were flight incidents, too. One of the service pilots undershot on landing and struck the runway verge, bending the aircraft a bit but managing to keep it on the runway. Generally the service tests went well.

Meanwhile, in 1970 the Gor'kiy aircraft factory started producing the MiG-25RB, starting with c/n 020ST03 (f/n 0603). The production aircraft was intended for clear-weather day/night PHOTINT, general-purpose and detailed SIGINT, day/night radar imaging in visual and instrument meteorological conditions and day/night bomb attacks in VMC and IMC. Reconnaissance was possible at altitudes up to 23,000 m (75,460 ft) and speeds of 2,500-3,000 km/h (1,552-1,863 mph) within a combat radius of 920 km (571 miles). It was possible to deliver bombs from up to 21,000 m (68,900 ft) and 2,500 km/h within a combat radius of 650 km (403 miles) while performing all kinds of reconnaissance tasks. After dropping the bombs the pilot was supposed to maintain a speed of at least Mach 2.25, performing the getaway manoeuvre with 60° bank in daylight conditions and 45° bank at night. Should the Peleng-D navigation suite fail during the bombing run, the strike could be performed in manual mode, making use of the Polyot-1I flight/navigation suite.

The baseline camera fit was identical to that of the MiG-25R (four A-70Ms and one A/E-10). Other options comprised two A-72 cameras with 150-mm (5.9 in) lenses for detail reconnaissance of a narrow strip of terrain, or a single A-87 with a 650-mm (25.6 in) lens. For ELINT duties, an SRS-4A (*izdeliye* 30A) or SRS-4B (*izdeliye* 30B) general-purpose SIGINT set was fitted; alternatively, the SRS-4V (*izdeliye* 30V) version could be fitted. The aircraft also carried an SPS-141 Siren'-1F active jammer.

The MiG-25RB became operational in December 1970 as the first of the reconnais-

Different versions of the MiG-25RB occasionally operated in pairs, complementing each other. Here, the lead aircraft ('09 Red') is a MiG-25RBK with a Koob-3 SIGINT set, while the wingman ('15 Red') is a MiG-25RBS with a Sablya-E SLAR revealed by the much larger dielectric panel.

sance/strike versions. Early production aircraft had a bomb load restricted to 2,000 kg (4,410 lb) and carried four FAB-500M-62 low-drag bombs under the fuselage. Later, wing pylons were added, doubling the bomb load. Four MBD3-U2 bomb racks were fitted – two in tandem on the fuselage centreline and one under each wing. (MBD = *mnogozam**kovyy** **bah**lochnyy der**zhah**tel'* – multiple beam-type rack; U = *oonifit-**see**rovannyy* – standardised. Thus, MBD3-U2 means 'MER, Group 3 (capable of carrying ordnance up to 500 kg/1,102 lb calibre), standardised, two-bomb version'.) They could carry four to eight 80-kg (176-lb) FotAB-100-80 flare bombs or 250-kg (551-lb) FAB-250 HE bombs, or eight FAB-500M-62 or FAB-500M-62T HE bombs. For combined reconnaissance/strike missions the aircraft carried four FAB-250 bombs on the belly MERs; no centreline drop tank could be carried in this case.

Late-production MiG-25RBs, starting with c/n N02022077, had the bomb load increased to 5,000 kg (11,020 lb) and could carry ten FAB-500M-62s (four in tandem pairs under the wings and six under the fuselage on modified MBD3-U2T MERs, the T standing for 'tandem'). However, it soon became obvious that this ordnance load was excessive, impairing speed and service ceiling drastically because of the extra drag and weight. Besides, wing loading was excessive at subsonic speeds and the air intake walls were subject to higher stress at speeds in excess of Mach 0.9, which could cause fatigue problems.

The fin tanks were deleted on late production aircraft in the mid-1970s, restricting fuel tankage to the wings and fuselage. The huge 5,300-litre drop tank also impaired performance a good deal; still it was rarely jettisoned when it ran dry. No bombs could be carried when the drop tank was fitted.

The MiG-25RB *et seq.* were equipped with the more accurate Peleng-DM navigation/bombing system. This included a more refined Orbita-10 central processor and a DISS-7 Doppler speed/drift sensor system.

The thrust of the MiG-25RB's massive engines enabled it to perform sustained level flight, albeit with deceleration, at altitudes above its nominal service ceiling. The effective level flight ceiling in full afterburner with 3,300 kg (7,275 lb) of fuel remaining at the end of the flight mode was 26,000-27,000 m (85,300-88,580 ft). The MiG-25RB could exceed Mach 2.4 for 15 minutes; a Mach 2.65-2.83 dash was also possible but was not to exceed five minutes. Cruising time at speeds below Mach 2.4 was unlimited.

MiG-25RB deliveries to VVS units commenced in 1970. This version stayed in production for two years until superseded by more sophisticated versions in 1972. The NATO reporting name was *Foxbat-B*.

To meet VVS requirements, a version designated **MiG-25RBK** was developed, the K referring to the Koob-3 (*izdeliye* K-3) detailed SIGINT suite. Work on this version started concurrently with the MiG-25R, since the latter's mission equipment could detect pulse-Doppler radars but could not transmit data to ground command centres. In contrast, the Koob-3 suite could pinpoint the location of enemy transmitters (both pulsed and continuous), define their class and relay intelligence immediately via data link while storing it in a digital recorder for later analysis. The 'cube' weighed several hundred kilos and was too bulky to install on an interchangeable pallet, like the SRS-4 packs. Hence the aircraft's nose had to be redesigned; the cameras were deleted and the camera ports faired over.

The MiG-25RBK prototype, '305 Blue' (c/n 020 SO 05, f/n 0305), was converted from a very early MiG-25R in the summer of 1970 and underwent rigorous testing in 1971-73. once the State acceptance

Three-quarters rear view of a MiG-25RBK. Note the late-style elongated brake parachute housing nestled between the huge nozzles of the R15B-300 engines.

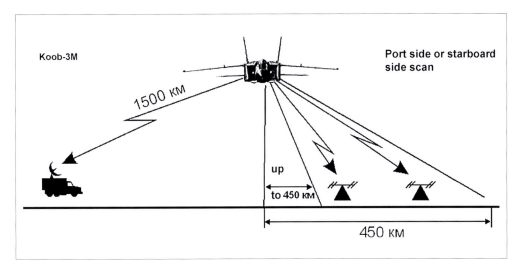

A diagram showing how the MiG-25RBK's Koob-3M SIGINT set could detect emitters within 450 km (279 miles) of the aircraft's track (either to port or to starboard). The intelligence was relayed via data link to a receiver/processing station situated up to 1,500 km (931 miles) away.

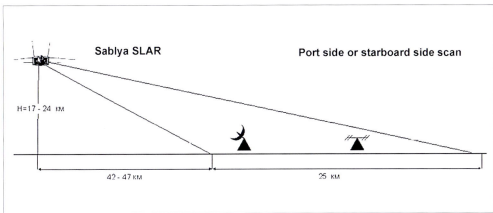

A diagram showing how the MiG-25RBS flying at 17,000-24,000 m (55,770-78,740 ft) could map a strip of land 25 km (15.5 miles) wide beginning at 42-47 km (26-29 miles) from the aircraft's track (either to port or to starboard).

A fine study of MiG-25RBK '55 Red' on final approach.

trials had been successfully completed, the MiG-25RBK entered production in Gor'kiy in 1973, staying in production until 1980; the product code was initially *izdeliye* 02K but was later changed to *izdeliye* 51 to enhance security. Production aircraft had an upgraded Koob-3M (*izdeliye* K-3M) SIGINT suite, an SPS-143 Siren'-3F active jammer and similar armament to the MiG-25RB. Late-production MiG-25RBKs featured air intake upper walls of greater area, a more elongated brake parachute housing and an SPO-15 Beryoza radar homing and warning system (*sis**te**ma predooprezh**den**iya ob obloo**chen**ii* – 'irradiation warning system') replacing the earlier SPO-10 Sirena-3M radar warning receiver. The SPO-15 not only alerted the pilot that he was being 'painted' by enemy radars but also displayed the bearing, type of radar and its operating mode. Starting in 1981, MiG-25RBKs were retrofitted with more modern reconnaissance equipment.

A slightly downgraded export version of the MiG-25RBK was developed for 'friendly nations', featuring less sophisticated guidance and weapons control systems. According to press reports, more than 30 MiG-25Rs (*sic*) were delivered to Algeria, eight to Iraq, five to Libya, eight to Syria and six to India. Three or four MiG-25RBKs briefly saw service with the Bulgarian Air Force but were soon exchanged for MiG-23BN *Flogger-H*

fighter-bombers because Bulgaria had no real use for Mach 2+ reconnaissance/strike aircraft.

When the synthetic aperture radar was invented in the early 1960s it opened the possibility to obtain radar imagery of comparable quality to traditional photos. As early as 1963, having verified the basic design principles of such a radar on flying testbeds, the Moscow Research Institute of Instrument Engineering named after Vladimir V. Tikhomirov (NIIP – *Na**ooch**no-is**sle**dovatel'skiy insti**toot** pri**bor**ostro**yen**iya*) proposed developing a SLAR tailored to the design of the Ye-155R. It took two years for the idea to ripen, and in 1965 the VVS issued a specific operational requirement for a SLAR-equipped spyplane.

Development of the **Sa**blya E SLAR (Sabre E, or *izdeliye* 122) lasted nearly seven years. It was a monobloc unit of advanced modular design and the first Soviet radar capable of generating photographic quality imagery. The reconnaissance/strike version equipped with the Sablya E radar was designated, quite logically, **MiG-25RBS**. The prototype, '304 Blue' (c/n 020 SO 04, f/n 0304), was converted from a MiG-25R in the summer of 1970. The new version could be identified by two large dielectric panels on the sides of the nose – much larger than on previous versions. The MiG-25RBS was fitted with an SPS-142 Siren'-2F jammer and had

The flight line of a reconnaissance regiment. MiG-25RBS '14 Red' is nearest to camera, with MiG-25RBK '36 Red' beyond it.

Three reconnaissance *Foxbats* parked with drop tanks attached, with MiG-25RBS '40 Blue' nearest to camera.

Two views of a retired MiG-25RBS ('09 Red') serving as an instructional airframe in the Tambov Technical School, Russia. Note the old-style short and pointed brake parachute housing.

MiG-25RBS '15 Red' fitted with a drop tank and ready for a mission.

A MiG-25RBS on a wintry hardstand in Lipetsk, with an AMK-24/56-131 air conditioner on a ZiL-131 chassis connected to it.

identical armament to the earlier strike version. No aerial cameras were fitted. The radar imagery was processed on the ground in a specially equipped van. The SLAR could detect parked aircraft, trains and ships and visualise the condition of bridges and similar structures.

After passing State acceptance trials in 1972-73 the MiG-25RBS entered production in 1973 as *izdeliye* 02S; this code was subsequently changed to *izdeliye* 52. The MiG-25RB, 'RBK and 'RBS officially entered service in keeping with two Council of Ministers directives issued on 13th April and 18th December 1972. Production of the MiG-25RBS continued until 1977; some aircraft were later refitted with new ELINT gear. This time NATO recognised the aircraft as a different version, allocating the reporting name *Foxbat-D*.

Another reconnaissance/strike version that came into being concurrently with the previous two had the standard SRS-4A/SRS-4B SIGINT packs replaced with a more modern SRS-9 *Virazh* (Banked turn) general-purpose SIGINT set, aka *izdeliye* 31.

Hence the aircraft was designated **MiG-25RBV**. Several optional camera fits were available for this model. Once again the prototype, '303 Blue' (c/n 020 SO 03, f/n 0303), was converted from a MiG-25R in the summer of 1970, passing State acceptance trials in 1971-72. New-build MiG-25RBVs were manufactured in 1973-79 as *izdeliye* 02V; the first production aircraft was c/n N02008008. Late-production aircraft had a new SPS-151 **Lyu***tik* (Buttercup) active jammer replacing the SPS-141.

Confusingly, from the mid-1970s onwards the remaining original *Foxbat-B*s with SRS-4 SIGINT sets were also referred to in service as MiG-25RBVs. However, their factory code (*izdeliye* 02B) remained unchanged.

As mentioned earlier, to meet the Air Force's specific operational requirements the Mikoyan OKB had made provisions for high-altitude night PHOTINT missions when developing the Ye-155R. Two NAFA-MK-75 cameras designed by the Kazan' Optical & Mechanical Plant (which, like the Krasnogorsk plant, was abbreviated as KOMZ)

A diagram showing that the MiG-25RBV could photograph a 70-km (43.5-mile) strip of land, while the Virazh-1M SIGINT set could detect emitters within a swath 900 km (559 miles) wide.

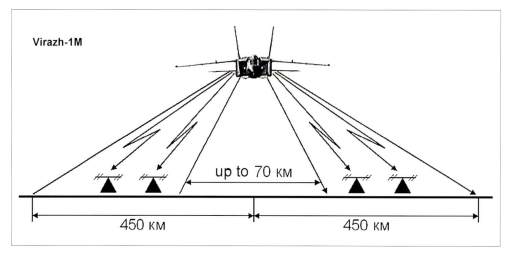

Virazh-1M

up to 70 KM

450 KM   450 KM

Left: This MiG-25RBV is another instructional airframe in the Tambov Technical School.

Below and bottom: This MiG-25RBV used to be on display at the now defunct museum at Moscow-Khodynka.

A technician cranks the hoist, raising the camera pallet, while another technician prepares to secure the six retaining latches. Note the staggered position of the camera ports.

could be installed in the standard camera nose with the optical axes slightly tilted aft. Four to ten FotAB-100-80 or FotAB-100-140 flare bombs were carried on MERs under the fuselage; they were released over the target area by the Peleng navigation system, the initial flash triggering a sensor that opened the camera shutters. The burn time of a single bomb was sufficient for two exposures. The NAFA-MK-75 had a lens with a high aperture ratio (1:3.5) and shutter speeds between 1/25 and 1/80. When extra sensitive film was loaded it was possible to shoot in dusk without the benefit of flare bombs. The aircraft could also be fitted with the SRS-9 Virazh SIGINT suite. The night PHOTINT version was designated **MiG-25RBN** (*noch**noy*** – night, used attributively).

Yet it was obvious that the night PHOTINT version offered no great advantage. Firstly, the results simply weren't worth the effort; the very complex mission yielded just 16 exposures of rather poor quality, and photography was only possible in clear weather. Secondly, in peacetime, night photography was only possible over sparsely populated areas because the bright

flashes of the exploding flare bombs could cause panic among civilians, to say nothing of the falling splinters that could cause bodily harm or damage to property. Therefore, the night PHOTINT version was excluded from the State acceptance trials programme.

In the course of the trials programme the shutter operating logic was changed. The shutters opened in advance and closed right after the flash; thus, the burn time of the flare bombs was used better. Despite being scheduled to begin right after the State acceptance trials of the basic MiG-25R and be completed as soon as possible, the MiG-25RBN's test programme was not completed until the MiG-25RB came into being.

In 1979 the Mikoyan OKB and GNIKI VVS began State acceptance trials of yet another reconnaissance/strike model – the **MiG-25RBT**. This differed from the MiG-25RBV in having the Virazh SIGINT pack replaced by a *Tan**gazh*** (Pitch, as an aircraft's motion) general-purpose SIGINT pack, hence the T. The Tangazh module (*izdeliye* 33) was lighter and more reliable; it also had a wider range of detectable radars and their location could be pinpointed when

'21 Red', a 931st GvORAP MiG-25RBT, at Werneuchen AB in East Germany. Note the 'Excellent aircraft' maintenance award badge.

'04 Red', a 164th GvORAP MiG-25RBT parked in front of a concrete blast deflector at Brzeg AB, Poland.

MiG-25RBT '61 Red' comes in to land at a German airbase on a bleak day in the early 1990s.

Front view of a 47th GvORAP MiG-25RBT ('40 Red') at Shatalovo AB, showing the camera ports.

Above: Two more views of the same aircraft, showing the dielectric panels concealing the antennas of the Tangazh SIGINT suite. An APA-5D on a Ural-4320 chassis provides ground power.

Right: A diagram showing that the MiG-25RBT's Tangazh SIGINT set could detect hostile emitters within a swath 900 km (559 miles) wide.

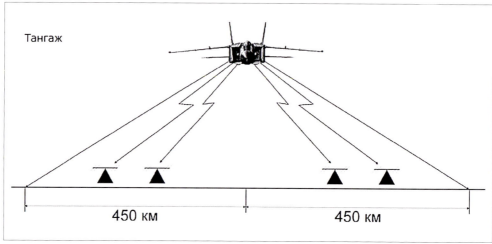

Тангаж

450 км   450 км

Above and left: Three-quarters rear views of MiG-25RBT '40 Red', the rear fuselage showing some signs of operational wear and tear.

Below: 931st GvORAP MiG-25RBT '57 Red' on the flight line at Werneuchen AB.

the recorded intelligence was processed post-flight. The aircraft featured the new SRO-1P *Parol'* (Password, aka *izdeliye* 62) IFF transponder and the SPO-15 Beryoza RHAWS. Known in-house as *izdeliye* 02T, the MiG-25RBT was produced by the Gor'kiy aircraft factory in 1980-82; some MiG-25RBVs were also updated to this standard. Once again the reporting name was *Foxbat-B*.

A mid-life update (MLU) programme for the MiG-25RBS was launched in 1981. The Sablya SLAR, which was extremely troublesome, gave place to the new-generation **Shom**pol (Ramrod, aka *izdeliye* M202) SLAR; hence the updated aircraft were redesignated

MiG-25RBSh or *izdeliye* 02Sh. The Shompol had a resolution two to three times better than the Sablya; besides, it allowed the aircraft to work at any altitude between 300 and 23,000 m (980-75,460 ft), whereas the Sablya could not operate below 17,000 m (55,770 ft). Also, the new SLAR had a moving target selection (MTS) mode and a combined mapping/MTS mode. The aircraft featured new Peleng-2, RSBN-10S (SHORAN) and A-711 Klystron (LORAN) navigation systems. Part of the fleet was upgraded in due course; outwardly the MiG-25RBSh could be discerned from the MiG-25RBS by the new-style brake parachute housing and the presence of dielectric ECM blisters on the air intake

Opposite and above: MiG-25RBT '40 White' seen during a practice sortie.

Below: MiG-25RBT '54 Red' was an 11th ORAP aircraft operating from Neu-Welzow AB, Germany, in 1991-92.

Opposite page:
Many MiG-25RBSs were upgraded to MiG-25RBSh standard, exemplified here by '08 Red'.

A MiG-25RBSh at Kubinka AB. The ECM antenna blisters on the air intakes were one of this version's external distinguishing features from the MiG-25RBS.

This page:
MiG-25RBSh '76 Red' parked in front of a welded steel blast deflector at the Air Force's test centre in Akhtoobinsk shows off its four-tone tactical camouflage.

trunks. As with the predecessor, the reporting name was *Foxbat-D*.

In 1981 it was the MiG-25RBK's turn to get an MLU. The Koob-3M SIGINT suite was replaced by an up-to-date Shar-25 (Ball, or Balloon) detailed SIGINT system (*izdeliye* F-25S). The aircraft received the same navigation system upgrades and was also fitted with active jammers and chaff/flare dispensers.

The word 'shar' begins with the letter Sh; however, this suffix letter was by then allocated to the Shompol-equipped MiG-25RBSh and could not be used. Therefore, the latest version received the 'out-of-

sequence' designation **MiG-25RBF**, or *izdeliye* 02F; the F was borrowed from the mission system's product code. Curiously, many Western publications misidentify the Soviet/Russian Air Force MiG-25RBFs stationed in (former East) Germany and Poland as MiG-25RBSh's, despite the fact that the two versions differ markedly in appearance! The key to this puzzle is that the Russian technicians, when asked by Western spotters about the aircraft type in the days of the Russian pullout, said these aircraft were MiG-25RBSh's – earnestly believing they were RBSh's *because they had the Shar-25 system*! Even the people working on the

Top: A MiG-25RBF becomes airborne with the engines in maximum afterburner.

Above: MiG-25RBF '51 Red' takes off with a drop tank.

Above: 11th ORAP MiG-25RBF '58 Red' is seen on final approach to Neu-Welzow. Note the deflected intake lower lips.

Below: 931st GvORAP MiG-25RBF '38 Red' was the sole camouflaged *Foxbat* stationed in Germany. Here the aircraft is pushed back into its hardened aircraft shelter (HAS) at Werneuchen.

actual aircraft don't take the trouble to find out the correct designation sometimes...

The aircraft could be outwardly discerned from the MiG-25RBK by the two small dielectric panels located low on each side of the nose in lieu of camera ports. The Shar-25 suite was speedy and could work in a jumbled radio signal environment, picking out assorted transmitters. It could detect state-of-the-art radars with a complex emission spectrum and quickly relay data to ground command centres. The MiG-25RBK to RBF and MiG-25RBS to RBSh upgrades were done at VVS aircraft repair plants when the aircraft were due for a major overhaul.

A small batch of eight MiG-25RBVs was modified for RINT duties, superseding the Yak-25RR and the Yak-28RR *Brewer-D*. The MiG-25RR had a higher service ceiling than both of the Yakovlev types and, importantly, could slip through the contaminated area quicker, reducing pilot exposure. Designated **MiG-25RR** (*radiatsionnyy razvedchik* – RINT aircraft), the aircraft carried a *Vysota* (Altitude) mission equipment suite, including a FUKA air sampling pod intended for detecting radioactive particles in the atmosphere at high altitude. This equipment had originally been designed by the Yakovlev OKB for the abovementioned types; Mikoyan OKB engineers modified it, adapting the equipment to the *Foxbat*. In the 1970s and 1980s MiG-25RRs repeatedly flew sorties along the Sino-Soviet border, monitoring Chinese nuclear tests. These aircraft were later fitted with upgraded RINT equipment.

Overall, more than 220 MiG-25s were manufactured in various reconnaissance/strike versions; the last aircraft left the production line in 1982.

It may be mentioned that two-seat trainer versions of the MiG-25 were developed in the late 1960s to facilitate pilot training – largely thanks to insistent demands from the test pilots and instructors. The designers used a stepped-tandem arrangement, the instructor's cockpit being housed in a redesigned nose ahead of and below the standard cockpit which seated the trainee. This simple but effective solution afforded an excellent field of view for both crew members. In addition to controls and flight instruments, the instructor's cockpit was fitted with a failure simulation panel so that the instructor could throw in simulated malfunctions for the trainee and see how the latter would cope. The interceptors and reconnaissance/strike versions had separate trainer variants; the trainer for the MiG-25RB *et seq.* was designated **MiG-25RU** (*razvedchik oochebnyy* – reconnaissance aircraft, trainer) or *izdeliye* 39. The MiG-25RU lacked the SUSAB bomb delivery system and the Peleng-DR navigation system. Development was completed in 1970; the prototype (c/n 390SA01) made its first flight at Gor'kiy-Sormovo on 20th March 1971. Service trials began in September 1971, and full-scale production followed in 1972; the production run was small, totalling 50 examples. The only visible difference from the MiG-25PU interceptor trainer was the absence of missile pylons (unlike the reconnaissance versions, the MiG-25RU had wings with a kinked leading edge typical of the interceptors).

Opposite page:

Here the same aircraft taxies out for a practice sortie. The crude camouflage was applied locally.

'20 Red', another camouflaged MiG-25RBF, belonged to the 47th GvORAP and is pictured at its home base, Shatalovo AB, in the early 1990s.

Another 47th GvORAP MiG-25RBF in the static display during an 'open house' at Kubinka AB. Note the badge of Squadron 2 on the air intake showing a cheetah (a reference to the MiG-25's speed) leaping across the globe.

This page:

'32 Red', a MiG-25RU trainer belonging to the 47th GvORAP, is refuelled by a TZ-22 articulated fuel truck at Shatalovo AB. The stepped arrangement of the cockpits is clearly visible.

Opposite page:
The flight line at Shatalovo, with MiG-25RBT '46 Red' in the foreground and MiG-25RU '32 Red' behind.

MiG-25RBT '46 Red' and MiG-25RU '32 Red' are 'tucked away for the night' at Shatalovo.

This page:
A 931st GvORAP crew boards MiG-25RU '02 Red' for a training sortie at Werneuchen AB.

MiG-25RU '36 White' shows how weathered the paintwork on the *Foxbat* could become. The darker paint on the forward fuselage has retained its original colour because the cockpit section is under wraps when the aircraft is parked for an extended time.

RECONNAISSANCE *FOXBATS* IN ACTION

As mentioned earlier, the 47th GvORAP of the Moscow Military District based at Shatalovo AB led the way. This unit, which bore the honorary appellation *Borisovskiy* for its part in liberating the Belorussian city of Borisov during the Great Patriotic War, and was awarded the Suvorov Order and the Order of the Red Banner of Combat, was traditionally the first to introduce new reconnaissance aircraft types. In October 1969 the General Staff of the Soviet Armed Forces issued a directive ordering that one squadron of the 47th GvORAP (then equipped with the Yak-27R *Mangrove*) be converted to the MiG-25R. The choice fell on Sqn 1, which had the best level of flight training; a group of 16 pilots was selected for conversion. At the end of the year they studied the aircraft in Gor'kiy and the R15B-300 engine in Moscow; in April 1970 they took additional theoretical training in Lipetsk. The first three brand-new MiG-25Rs ('40 Blue' through '42 Blue', c/ns 020SE01, 020SE04 and 020SE05 respectively) arrived at Shatalovo AB on 9th or 10th June; after a period of ground training the unit's pilots made their first solo flights in the MiGs on 16th July. (Of these three, '42 Blue' crashed on 22nd July 1971, the pilot ejecting safely, while '41 Blue' was written off after overrunning at Shatalovo and shearing off the nose

gear. The local maintenance shop did return the machine to airworthy status after more than a year's work, but the aircraft had been 'bent', which affected its handling to such an extent that Mikoyan OKB test pilot Aleksandr V. Fedotov declared the aircraft unfit for service after making a single flight in it.)

A turning point in the MiG-25R's career came when it actually saw combat on the Middle Eastern theatre of operations. Being on friendly terms with the Arab nations, the Soviet Union could not remain unperturbed when Israel defeated Egypt in the Six-Day War (5th-11th June 1967). In late January 1970 Egyptian President Gamal Abdel Nasser paid a secret visit to Moscow, asking for assistance in re-equipping the Egyptian armed forces. Specifically this included training military specialists, particularly SAM crews, and building up an effective air defence system.

Nasser's request was granted immediately. As early as February 1970 Egyptian troops began arriving in the USSR by the brigade to take their training, and deliveries of the latest Soviet military equipment began. The headquarters of all Egyptian Army units, right down to battalion level, had Soviet military advisors attached. In March-April 1970 Soviet SAM battalions and fighter units moved into Egypt to provide protection for targets of importance, such as the Aswan dam, the seaport of Alexandria, air bases, army depots and factories. How-

MiG-25RB '57 Blue', one of the four 47th GvORAP aircraft seconded to Det 63, sits in front of a HAS at Cairo-West AB in 1971.

ever, the USSR did not stop at that; Soviet military experts took part in planning the operations aimed at liberating the Sinai Peninsula annexed by Israel. The Egyptian Army was to cross the Suez Canal and move on into the Sinai. However, thorough reconnaissance was necessary, since the Israelis had established a mighty defensive line along the Suez – the supposedly impregnable Bar-Lev line.

A new Arab-Israeli war was brewing. The Soviet leaders were well aware that the Egyptian armed forces were in no shape to take on the Israelis alone, even though it had been rebuilt by 1971 with massive Soviet aid. However, direct Soviet involvement in a Middle Eastern conflict (the way many Arab leaders would like it!) was out of the question, as it was guaranteed to trigger the Third World War. Therefore, the Soviet government decided to send a special reconnaissance task force flying MiG-25Rs to Egypt. The Ministry of Aircraft Industry was instrumental to this decision.

At the time the MiG-25 programme was in limbo. The trials were dragging out, with many problems requiring urgent solution, and the fatal crash of PVO Aviation C-in-C Gen. Anatoliy L. Kadomtsev in a MiG-25P in April 1969 certainly did not help. The military were becoming pessimistic about the MiG-25, and the decision whether it was going to be accepted was nowhere in sight. It was then that Vice-Minister of Aircraft Industry Aleksey V. Minayev (who, being a former Mikoyan OKB employee, had taken part in the development of the MiG-25 and cared about the aircraft) suggested trying it out in the Middle East. The military were also interested in finding out what the MiG-25 could do and jumped at the rare opportunity to test it in actual combat.

There was no point in sending the MiG-25P interceptor to the Middle East. Firstly, one or two aircraft could not save the Egyptian air defence force, and the USSR could not afford to send more since it was guaranteed to attract attention in the West and be regarded as direct intervention. Secondly, the MiG-25P was most effective at long range and high altitude, and the Middle Eastern TO was simply too cramped for it.

Besides, there was the question of enemy tactics; the situation called for numerous highly manoeuvrable light fighters, rather than a handful of heavy interceptors, to counter the Israeli aircraft. Thus, the Soviet leaders decided that sending four reconnaissance aircraft would do a lot more good, since they could furnish tactical information rapidly and, importantly, boost the morale of the Egyptian forces.

In the summer of 1970 a task force of 70 men headed by Minayev was formed at GNIKI VVS. This included the cream of the specialists from GNIKI VVS, the Air Force's 4th TsBP i PLS and the 47th GvORAP. Mikoyan OKB and aircraft industry employees who had participated in refining the aircraft and knew it well were also included.

The task force also included six experienced pilots (mostly VVS pilots); the Mikoyan OKB was also represented by MiG-25 deputy project chief Lev G. Shengelaya, Ishchenko and Yuriy F. Polooshkin.

The group of test engineers included highly experienced men from the Gor'kiy aircraft factory (headed by Goryunov), the Tumanskiy engine design bureau (headed by Groozdev) and the Salyut plant producing the R15B-300 turbojet. RPKB, which was responsible for the Peleng navigation system, sent engineer Boorov, and VNIIRA was represented by radio navigation systems expert Andjian. The actual rank and status of each man in the team was kept secret, and the group was closely guarded by Egyptian commandos at all times after arriving in Egypt.

A few words need to be said about the pilots involved in the mission. Vladimir G. Gordiyenko (who was then the Gor'kiy aircraft factory's chief test pilot) flew nearly all production MiG-25s and taught service pilots to handle the aircraft. GNIKI VVS test pilot Col. Nikolay I. Stogov, pilot V. Uvarov (4th TsBP i PLS) and 47th GvORAP pilots Capt. N. P. Borshchov, Capt. Yuriy V. Marchenko, Maj. N. P. Choodin and Capt. Krasnogorskiy were all seasoned airmen. Test pilot (1st Class) Col. Aleksandr S. Bezhevets, a man renowned for his resolve and command skills, was put in charge of the group. Also, he was second to none in knowing the MiG-25, having flown the first Ye-155 prototypes back in 1965. Bezhevets was faced with the daunting task of keeping the large and motley team organised. In the first days of the task force's stay in Egypt it was directed by Air Marshal Aleksandr N. Yefimov (First Deputy C-in-C of the VVS who later went on to become C-in-C) and Lt.-Gen. Grigoriy U. Dol'nikov, deputy chief Air Force advisor in Egypt.

Two 'pure reconnaissance' MiG-25Rs (c/ns 020SE01 and 020SE04, f/ns 0501 and 0504) and two MiG-25RB reconnaissance/strike aircraft (c/ns 020SL02 and 020ST01, f/ns 0402 and 0601) were selected among the early production aircraft undergoing tests at GK NII VVS. The tech staff was familiar with these aircraft, which simplified maintenance. For PHOTINT duties the aircraft could carry two different camera sets composed of A-72, A-87 and A/E-10 cameras, as well as interchangeable SRS-4A/SRS-4B SIGINT packs.

The location where the group was to operate was kept secret until the last moment. The first clue was the medical examination which all the pilots had to pass to make sure they were fit for service in hot and dry climatic zones. The 'hot and dry' bit suggested Africa; this was confirmed soon enough when the top brass informed that the group was to 'extend international help' to the Arab Republic of Egypt.

Training was completed and everything set to go by late September 1970. But then Nasser died on 28th September; Anwar

Sadat, his successor, seemed more intent on negotiating than waging a war. A change in Egypt's political course seemed probable, and the trip was postponed. However, Sadat confirmed that Egypt was firm in its resolve to win back the land seized by Israel, and the programme went ahead as planned.

In March 1971 the group was ordered to pack their bags and redeploy to Egypt on the double. To save time the personnel and the four aircraft were to be airlifted by Soviet Air Force An-12 and An-22 Antey (*Cock*) transports. But even with the wings, tail unit and engines removed the MiGs would not fit into the An-22's cargo cabin – they were a couple of inches too wide and too high. The fuselage width was OK but the mainwheels got stuck in the Antey's cargo door.

When there's a will, there's a way. Thinking fast, someone suggested reversing the main gear struts so that the mainwheels faced inboard instead of outboard. Someone else suggested temporarily fitting MiG-21 mainwheels. They were strong enough to take the weight of the stripped-down aircraft but much smaller than the MiG-25's standard mainwheels, enabling the aircraft to go through the cargo door, though it was a very tight squeeze.

The group, designated the 63rd OAO (ot**del'**nyy a**viaotryad** – Independent Air Detachment, or Det 63), was based at Cairo-West AB. For security reasons all members of the group wore Egyptian uniforms with no rank insignia. Det 63 reported directly to Col.-Gen. V. V. Okunev, the top Soviet military advisor in Egypt; Maj.-Gen. Semyon I. Kharlamov, HSU, was responsible for tactical planning and objective setting. Aleksey V. Minayev and Lev G. Shengelaya monitored the group's operations from the manufacturer's side.

The Egyptians had already built huge hardened aircraft shelters (HASs) for the MiGs. Using the shelters, the highly skilled Soviet technicians managed to reassemble the aircraft in a few days. In the meantime Israeli Defence Force/Air Force (IDF/AF) aircraft attacked the airfield several times, which caused the air defences at Cairo-West to be reinforced with S-75 and S-125 SAM batteries. The shelters containing the MiGs were further protected by five ZSU-23-4 Shilka quadruple 23-mm (.90 calibre) self-propelled AA guns manned by Soviet crews. The airfield itself was guarded by Soviet soldiers who built machine-gun emplacements and put up barbed wire fences around the perimeter; as it were, the Egyptians were only responsible for guarding the outskirts of the field. Finally, the assembled and checked aircraft were wheeled over to the revetments previously occupied by Egyptian Air Force Tu-16KS-1 cruise missile carriers.

It was just as well that the task force was so painstaking about security measures. It turned out that the locals, for all their friendly attitude, could not be trusted to keep their mouths shut. Egyptian officers never gave security a second thought, and

having them participate in mission planning and support meant that the Israelis were aware of the group's plans almost before the meeting adjourned. A few days after the task force moved to Cairo the local paper *Al-Akhram* raised a ballyhoo, carrying a banner headline 'New aircraft at Cairo-West air base!' For sheer effect the paper labelled the aircraft 'X-500', but the accompanying pictures left no doubts as to their identity (and origin).

The Soviet task force was very worried indeed by how fast the Israelis got news of its planned sorties. This forced a change in the cooperation procedures with the Egyptians to stop possible breaches of security. A meeting chaired by Gen. Okunev resolved that from then on all work of Det 63 would be done only by Soviet personnel.

Ensuring flight safety turned out to be a major difficulty, too. To avoid encounters with IDF/AF aircraft special air routes had to be developed, ensuring that the MiG-25s were protected by SAMs at all times during climb and descent. The pilots also perfected a steep landing approach (not unlike the 'Khe Sanh tactical approach' used by the USAF in Vietnam) and devised evasive manoeuvres for escaping missiles. During descent the MiG-25 boasted a thrust/weight ratio better than 1; in contrast, Israeli McDonnell F-4E Phantom IIs and Dassault Mirage IIICJs had a ratio of 0.6 to 0.7.

The first flights over Egyptian territory began in late April 1971. During this period, mission profiles were drawn up, cameras tried out and navigation computers adjusted and programmed. Test pilot Vladimir Gordiyenko was the first to go up. During that sortie the SIGINT pack recorded that, in addition to Israeli radars located in the Sinai Peninsula, the aircraft had been 'painted' by a US Navy destroyer's radar and a British surveillance radar located on a mountain top on Cyprus. Later, Yuriy Marchenko and Aleksandr Bezhevets also started flying sorties. These sorties had one curious feature. To ensure the best possible picture quality the automatic flight control system had to follow the predetermined route very closely, using landmarks – which were unavailable in the desert. Hence, the famous pyramids of the Valley of the Pharaohs were used as landmarks, causing the pilots to refer to these missions as 'guided tours'.

The preparations were completed in May 1971 and the group was ready for combat sorties. Missions were planned painstakingly. The pilot would start the engines while the aircraft was still in the HAS, then run a systems check and taxi out for take-off. Then he carefully positioned the aircraft on the runway because the holding position was clearly defined and entered into the SAU-155R1 automatic flight control system (sist**em**a avtoma**tich**eskovo oopravl**en**iya). This was the starting point of the mission; from there the pilot proceeded, strictly observing radio silence – the pilots were allowed to go on air only in an emergency.

For security reasons the MiGs would take off without warning before some Egyptian could run off at the mouth that a sortie was planned. Cairo-West ATC would be 'officially' advised that nothing more serious than a routine engine check or taxi trials was cooking. As a result, the first unexpected (and unauthorised) take-off caused real panic among the Egyptians.

The *Foxbats* always operated in pairs. This increased mission success probability while giving the pilots that extra bit of confidence. Should one aircraft go down because of a critical systems failure (or be shot down – Egypt and Israel were officially at war, after all), the other pilot could report the crash and indicate the whereabouts, helping the SAR group.

Flying over enemy territory involved cruising at full military power for about 40 minutes. The air temperature in the engine inlet ducts peaked at 320°C (608°F); the aircraft skin was not much colder either (303°C/577°F). By then, the Tumanskiy OKB had extended engine running time in full afterburner from three to eight minutes and then to 40 minutes. Thus, virtually all sorties could be flown at maximum thrust; the R15B-300 turbojets proved reliable enough and gave no problems in the hot Egyptian climate.

Initially the MiG-25 used special T-6 grade jet fuel with a high boiling point which was unavailable in Egypt. To supply Det 63 with this exotic fuel, Soviet tankers would sail from Soviet seaports to Alexandria, whence the fuel was delivered to Cairo by tanker lorries.

The Israelis were really angered by the MiG-25's overflights and started a veritable hunt for the aircraft, but the prey invariably got away. Yet the Israelis had an excellent SIGINT operation running, and calling in Egyptian fighters by radio to provide air cover would be an open invitation for the enemy to come in and try to shoot the MiG down. Since the Soviet pilots maintained radio silence, the Israelis had no alternative but to circle over Cairo-West AB, waiting for the *Foxbats* to line up for take-off.

Even then, they were out of luck. As the Israeli fighters moved in to attack they were immediately engaged by a flight of Egyptian Air Force MiG-21MFs flying top cover (these were summoned in advance from another airbase). After receiving word that the Soviet pilots were ready two of the MiG-21s streaked over the runway, followed immediately by the MiG-25s, a second pair of MiG-21s protecting the rear. In a few minutes the *Foxbats* would accelerate to Mach 2.5 and go 'up, up and away'.

Missions were flown at maximum speed and 17,000-23,000 m (55,770-75,460 ft). At this rate, no one could keep up with the MiG-25, and it was just as well because the reconnaissance aircraft were unarmed. The fuel was burned off at a rate of 500 kg (1,102 lb) per minute, reducing all-up weight, and the aircraft would gradually accelerate to

Mach 2.8. Pilots recalled that the canopy became so hot it burned your fingers if you touched it. As the aircraft approached the target area the vertical and oblique cameras were operated automatically, photographing a strip of land 90 km (56 miles) wide on either side of the aircraft. To prevent malfunctioning of the delicate equipment the camera bay was air-conditioned with a temperature variance of no more than 7°C (12.6°F).

Apart from high temperatures, photography at high Mach numbers involved another difficulty – the camera moved rapidly with respect to the object. In a single second the MiG-25 would travel almost 1,000 m (3,280 ft); thus, very high shutter speeds were needed to get clear pictures. To compensate for camera movement special adapters with movable prisms were developed, allowing the object to be kept in focus. Certain photo and ciné shooting modes required the aircraft to keep a constant speed. Another complication was that the MiG-25 kept climbing as fuel burnoff reduced weight, reaching 22,000 m (72,180 ft) at the end of its target run. In addition to taking pictures, the MiG-25Rs and MiG-25RBs pinpointed Israeli radars, communications centres and ECM facilities.

The entire flight from Suez to Port Said took just 1.5 or 2 minutes. On the approach to Cairo-West the reconnaissance aircraft were met by the MiG-21MFs, which escorted them all the way down, patrolling over the

Soviet pilots who took part in the MiG-25R/RB's first Egyptian deployment in 1971-72 pose for a photo with one of the aircraft involved; test pilot Aleksandr S. Bezhevets is in the middle.

airfield until the Soviet aircraft were safely in their shelters.

After losing several aircraft to SAMs the Israelis gave up trying to bomb the base, but the confrontation continued. In September 1971 an IDF/AF aircraft flying combat air patrol near Cairo-West was shot down by an Egyptian SAM. The Israelis retaliated by raiding the SAM sites, knocking out two of them with AGM-45 Shrike anti-radar missiles; the Soviet men and officers manning the sites were killed. This led the Soviet command to take additional protective measures for Det 63. In October 1971 special underground hangars were built for the MiG-25s at Cairo-West. These shelters could survive a direct hit of a 500-kg (1,102-lb) bomb and were fitted with all necessary communications and equipment. Pre-flight checks and routine maintenance, including engine run-up, were done underground and the aircraft only left the shelter immediately before take-off.

The MiG-25s flew two sorties per month. As they covered all of the Suez Canal area and went on to explore the Sinai Peninsula, the sorties grew longer, requiring a drop tank to be carried occasionally; with drop tank the aircraft's range exceeded 2,000 km (1,242 miles). The MiGs brought back hundreds of yards of film with valuable information, which was developed and sent to the intelligence section of the chief military advisor's HQ for analysis. The excellent pictures snapped from 20,000 m (65,620 ft) showed not only buildings and structures but also vehicles and even groups of people. Camouflaged materiel dumps and shelters were also visible. The SIGINT equipment helped to reveal a camouflaged ECM facility near Jebel Umm-Mahas and pinpoint Israeli air defence radars and SAM sites.

Det 63 continued to operate successfully. The MiG-25s ventured still farther afield – that is, farther east, and by the winter of 1971 their routes took them over Israel. The Soviet pilots were not afraid of Israeli jets scrambling to intercept them, having encountered them before over the Sinai Desert – the F-4E and Mirage IIICJ were simply no match for the MiG-25. The Phantom was inferior in speed and ceiling; trying to line up for an attack it would often stall and flick into a spin. The Mirage did even worse, and at best the Israeli pilots managed only to get a glimpse of the intruder.

The Raytheon MIM-23 Hawk SAMs used by Israel were no great threat to the MiG-25 either, since the aircraft operated beyond their altitude range (12,200 m/40,030 ft). The MiGs' radar warning receiver often sensed that the aircraft was being 'painted' by enemy radars but no missile warning ensued. On discovering a SAM site the pilot would simply switch on the Siren' jammer and carry on with his business. The deep penetration flights continued into March 1972. The Israeli ambassador to the United Nations lodged a formal complaint after each occurrence but no action on this issue was ever taken by the UN.

The Israelis *did* have a reason to be nervous. Among the support equipment and other paraphernalia Det 63 had brought with them were bomb racks for the two MiG-25RBs and a supply of FAB-500M-62T low-drag bombs. Each aircraft could carry up to eight such bombs; after being released at high altitude they could sail through the air for miles and miles. However, the Soviet pilots' missions did not include bomb strikes.

As an excuse for their inability to intercept the elusive MiGs the Israeli air defences stated that 'the object was clocked at Mach 3.2'! However, the flight recorders of the MiGs showed there were no major deviations from the prescribed flight profile. Oh yes, the aircraft were *not* always flown 'by the book'. On one occasion Aleksandr Bezhevets exceeded the speed limit to get away from pursuing Phantoms. Other sources state that it was VVS pilot Krasnogorskiy who should walk away with the record (and get the ticket), as he reached 3,400 km/h (2,111 mph) in one of the sorties. This was dangerous because the airframe could be damaged by overheating, but careful inspection of the aircraft showed no obvious damage. Still, the pilots received an unambiguous 'debriefing' after this incident.

The MiG-25s had a good reliability record during the first Egyptian deployment, with very few failures, despite the fact that the aircraft still had its share of bugs. Still, each aircraft came complete with a double set of spares – just in case.

Nasty surprises did happen, after all. On one occasion Nikolay Stogov's aircraft suffered an engine flameout and began decelerating rapidly, forcing the pilot to radio for help. He was ordered to return to base immediately or land at the alternate airfield from where escort fighters scrambled. However, seconds later the engine revived spontaneously and Stogov proceeded with the mission as planned. The trouble was traced to a faulty fuel control unit which the electronic engine control system somehow managed to correct.

A more serious incident happened to Aleksandr Bezhevets, who was flying the first machine reassembled on arrival in Egypt. A main gear breaker strut failed on landing approach and the strut would not lock down. Bezhevets decided to make a two-point landing. Touching down at 290 km/h (180 mph), he kept the aircraft's weight off the damaged strut as long as possible. Finally the strut collapsed and the aircraft slewed, scraping a wingtip along the ground and coming to rest across the runway. The landing was made so skilfully that the aircraft suffered only superficial damage to the wingtip and was soon flying again after the wingtip and landing gear had been repaired. (Some sources claim that, minor as the damage was, the aircraft was nevertheless returned to the USSR for repairs and a substitute MiG-25R sent in.)

Soviet MiG-25RB pilots in VKK-6M pressure suits and GSh-6 pressure helmets pose for a photo at Cairo-West AB; Aleksandr Bezhevets is rightmost. The man in civvies in the centre was probably one of the Soviet advisors.

There were other failures, too. For example, Uvarov's aircraft suffered a cockpit air conditioner failure during the descent, which caused the cockpit to get unbearably hot. Still, the bravery and skill of the pilots and technicians and the availability of spares accounted for the fact that no lives or aircraft were lost in the course of the deployment.

The original aircrew of Det 63 returned to the USSR in April 1972; the aircraft stayed and were flown by a new group of 47th GvO-RAP pilots – Lt. (SG) Nikolay Levchenko, Lt.-Col. Miroshnichenko, Maj. Yashin, Maj. Krasnogorskiy and Capt. Mashtakov. There was also navigator Goor'yanov who programmed the navigation computers, and the tech staff came almost entirely from the 47th GvORAP. Until April 1972 the MiG-25s flew along the Suez Canal; now they started flying over Israeli-held territory east of the canal, even venturing over Israel itself by the end of the year. The accident rate remained very low. On one occasion the cockpit glazing of the aircraft flown by VVS pilot Yashin failed at high altitude during deceleration; the cockpit decompressed but the pressure suit and oxygen system performed flawlessly, enabling Yashin to land safely.

In all, the MiG-25R/RBs flew about 20 sorties over Israeli-held territory during their Egyptian tour; all but one of them were flown by pairs of aircraft. The MiGs brought back excellent pictures showing clearly the positions of Israeli troops along the Suez. The Egyptian high command was very impressed by the detail level of the photos because their own MiG-21RFs had cameras with a narrow field of view and much of the valuable detail was lost.

The only single-aircraft sortie performed by Det 63 was flown by Aleksandr Bezhevets over the Mediterranean along the boundary of Israeli territorial waters. The pilot fired his cameras in a banking turn, a reconnaissance practice hitherto unknown. The good lighting conditions, very clear air and highly sensitive film enabled a shutter speed of 1/800 which, together with the high contrast of the image, provided excellent results.

According to the mission profile the aircraft was not to come within 10-20 km (6.21-12.4 miles) of the Israeli border. However, the navigation specialists had forgotten about the high salinity of the Mediterranean and failed to make corrections to the Doppler speed and drift sensor inputs when programming the navigation computer. As a result the navigation error amounted to several kilometres (usually it doesn't exceed 1 km/0.62 miles) and the aircraft flew directly over the border for 3 nautical miles (5.5 km). According to Soviet military advisors, this flight impressed the Israeli leaders greatly, showing all too clearly that the air defence was too weak.

The MiG-25's combat success in the Middle East was excellent testimony to the aircraft's unique capabilities and operational reliability. The designers and the military now had all the proof they needed, and in December 1972 the aircraft was officially taken on strength by the Soviet Air Force and Air Defence Force.

As time passed, however, the Egyptian leaders grew at odds with the Soviet Union. The MiG-25's excellent performance made Egypt want to buy the type, and that request was turned down. As a result, the tension escalated, with Egyptian troops exercising uncomfortably close to the hangars where the MiG-25s were parked. It was decided to move the aircraft back to the USSR (the

Crimea Peninsula or the Caucasus region). In July 1972 President Sadat banished all Soviet military staff from the country, thus putting an end to Det 63's operations. After some negotiating it was decided to airlift the MiGs out of the country by An-22s, the way they had come. The Israelis never managed to shoot down a MiG-25 and thus prove that the USSR was involved. Yet, this was not the end of the 47th GvORAP's Egyptian saga, as you shall see.

In 1972 the MiG-25 was officially included into the Soviet Air Force inventory. This applied to three versions – the RBV, RBS and RBK.

In the summer of 1973 the 47th GvORAP had its hands full with the service evaluation of the MiG-25RB. The programme included maximum speed flights, ELINT sorties, bomb delivery from the stratosphere (this involved bombing the Polesskiy target range in Belorussia and making a refuelling stop in Baranovichi), drop tank separation and so on. This was a major effort; suffice it to say that hundreds of miles (!) of test equipment tapes had to be deciphered. At first the MiG-25s cracked Mach 1 at just 5,000 m (16,400 ft) as stipulated by the combat application technique; however, this immediately led to complaints and repercussions because lots of windows and even roofs in the nearby town of Roslavl' were getting shattered by the sonic boom. After this, the transition altitude was hastily increased to 10,000 m (32,810 ft). The drop tank separation tests were performed over the Barents Sea. Four MiG-25RBs flew the test missions from Olen'ya AB, a North Fleet Aviation base near Murmansk, on 1st August 1973. Taking off at ten-minute intervals, they climbed to 15,000 m (49,210 ft), maintaining radio silence, then accelerated to Mach 1.5 and headed for a designated area of the sea where the drop tanks were jettisoned when they ran dry. Nikolay Levchenko, by then in the rank of major, flew one of the aircraft and recalled that the separation was accompanied by *'such a kick to the aircraft's belly that it felt like the aircraft would break in two'*. In addition to the primary test mission, the MiG-25RBs conducted ELINT of the coastline. All the while the aircraft's equipment registered the operation of NATO radar pickets; also, a USAF Boeing RC-135 spyplane – clearly there for the occasion – was loitering at 7,000-9,000 m (22,965-29,530 ft). The *potential adversary* must have been well informed of the mission!

Also, at the time the 47th GvORAP's Sqn 2 also transitioned from the Yak-27R to the MiG-25RB. Apart from that, the unit participated in various exercises and was tasked with conversion training of Air Force big brass to the MiG-25.

Pretty soon the *Foxbats* returned to Egypt. On 6th October 1973 Egypt unleashed the 'October War of Liberation' (better known as the 'Holy Day War', or Yom Kippur War), hoping to regain the territory it had lost in 1967. At first the Egyptians did

very well, penetrating the Bar-Lev line and advancing into Israeli territory on the Sinai Peninsula. But then the tables were turned as Israel launched a counteroffensive, securing a beachhead on the west bank of the Suez Canal. Having no reliable information about the enemy, Egypt had no choice but to turn to the USSR for help again.

On 19th and 20th October Soviet Air Force An-12s and An-22s brought four MiG-25RBs, personnel, spares, support equipment and even fuel to Cairo-West AB. The new *ad hoc* reconnaissance unit was designated the 154th Independent Air Detachment (Det 154). Once again the aircraft, pilots and ground crews were supplied by the 47th GvORAP. This time the industry group headed by MAP representative Ryabenko included Ryazanov and Polooshkin (Mikoyan OKB), Lenivtsev (RPKB), Chief Designers Andjian and Nalivayko (VNIIRA), reps from Tumanskiy OKB and the Gor'kiy aircraft factory. Lt.-Col. N. Choodin was commander of the flying group, which also included Maj. V. Uvarov, Capt. Yu. Garmash, Maj. V. Kur'yata, Capt. S. Gur'yanov (navigator), Capt. V. Mashtakov, Capt. N. Levchenko and Capt. S. Bukhtiyarov.

The situation was very different from the previous deployment, with Israeli tanks advancing on Cairo at an average 10 km (6.2 miles) per day. Cannonade could be heard in Heliopolis, a suburb of Cairo, in the morning hours. Thus, as the MiGs were reassembled, flying them back to the USSR was considered as an emergency option in case the Israelis got too close for comfort. (As a last-ditch possibility the aircraft could be blown up to prevent them from falling into enemy hands if Cairo-West was overrun. The personnel would be evacuated by road to the Libyan border.)

This time the Soviet contingent, apart from Det 154, included only a handful of SAM crews, military advisors working under contract with the Egyptians and small logistics groups responsible for organising airlifts and restoring the ties with the Egyptian top command. The personnel of Det 154 lived in a ramshackle building with no amenities and facilities that one of the pilots mockingly dubbed 'Sheraton-Hilton'.

The first sortie was flown on 22nd October, four days before the UN-brokered ceasefire came into effect. That day Lt.-Gen. Dvornikov (Deputy Commander of the Moscow Military District aviation), one of the Soviet advisors, unexpectedly appeared at the base. Nobody knew the purpose of his visit. Producing a map with the flight route marked on it, he gave it to Choodin and ordered him to send a pair of MiG-25s on a reconnaissance sortie, stating bluntly: *'If they are not airborne thirty minutes from now, you may consider that your detachment is here in vain, and you will have to face the consequences'*. Of course, half an hour was not enough even to make a simple calculation of the route, never mind programming the navigation systems; still, orders must be obeyed. Capt. Levchenko and Maj. Uvarov were tasked with the important mission; the more experienced Uvarov flew as the wingman – a practice that became standard in Det 154. With the required navigation aids not yet in place at Cairo-West AB, there was no option but to maintain the prescribed headings for the prescribed time – maintaining radio silence all the way. The pair headed north to Alexandria, then turned east to Port Said, turned on the mission equipment and proceeded south over the Sinai as far as Karun Island before heading back to Cairo-West. The flight lasted 32 minutes.

The mission was successful; developing the film and printing the pictures took the rest of the day and all of the night. By dawn the Egyptian command had learned the worst, realising the scale of their losses; the Egyptian Army Chief of Staff was openly crying, looking at the images of burnt-out Egyptian tanks in the desert. In a nutshell, Egypt had missed the chance to win a solid combat victory. After that, the Soviet SAM crews pulled out speedily but the MiGs of Det 154 stayed for another year, leaving for home in May 1975. The last combat sortie was flown in December 1973; after that, each pilot made one or two practice flights per week to maintain proficiency. There was no open hostility towards the Soviets, but the Arabs would throw a spanner in the works whenever they could. For example, a Soviet tanker carrying fuel for Det 154 was denied permission to dock, spending a week at the roadstead in Alexandria; fuel shortages eventually caused the flights to stop altogether. This was the last Soviet involvement in a Middle Eastern conflict.

There was, however, one more conflict in which Det 154 nearly saw action. In August 1974 Greece and Turkey clashed in an armed conflict over the issue of Cyprus. Hence a pair of MiG-25RBs was to make several sorties from Cairo-West in the interests of the UN Security Council to determine the frontline between Greek and Turkish forces. Yet the Egyptians sabotaged the mission by not giving take-off clearance in timely fashion. The pilots waited and waited in the sweltering heat; eventually permission was granted but it was afternoon by then, and the failing light made the mission pointless. The sortie was not flown the next day either, and eventually the mission was called off; it was a US Air Force Lockheed SR-71A that provided the pictures.

The successful combat evaluation of the MiG-25R/RB boosted the morale of the aircraft industry as well, giving rise to the spate of reconnaissance/strike versions with new ELINT equipment which enhanced the aircraft's capabilities considerably. The engines' TBO was extended and their fuel efficiency improved. The modified R15BD-300 engines were also retrofitted by repair shops in some cases to replace R15B-300s that had run out of service life.

A Det 63 pilot receives congratulations from one of his colleagues after a successful reconnaissance sortie over Israel, with Egyptian officers standing beside.

Later the reconnaissance versions of the *Foxbat* saw service with units of the Belorussian, Central Asian, Leningrad, Siberian and Trans-Caucasian Military Districts. They were also stationed abroad full-time. The Group of Soviet Forces in Germany (renamed the Western Group of Forces in 1989) had two reconnaissance units equipped with the *Foxbat* in the 16th Air Army. First, the 931st GvORAP stationed at Werneuchen AB near Potsdam since 1969 received its first MiG-25RBs and MiG-25RUs in 1974 while retaining its Yak-28Rs and Yak-28Us. The fleet was periodically renewed as older aircraft were due for an overhaul. One of the unit's MiG-25RBFs, '38 Red' (c/n N02032317), had the distinction of being the sole *Foxbat* in the 16th Air Army to wear a tactical camouflage scheme; the others had the standard light grey finish. A 931st GvORAP MiG-25RU crashed immediately east of the base in 1978. Another example, MiG-25RB '26 Red' (c/n N02050740), had an accident at the base in 1979 and was airlifted to the Soviet Union by an An-22 for repairs in 1980. In May 1991, when the Soviet pullout from reunited Germany was in progress, the unit vacated the base, transferring some of the MiG-25s to Sqn 3 of the 11th ORAP stationed at Neu-Welzow AB near Cottbus. However, in July 1992 these aircraft also departed to Russia.

Starting in early 1974, MiG-25RBs were also deployed with the North Group of Forces stationed in Poland, equipping a squadron of the 164th GvORAP stationed at Brzeg AB (pronounced 'bzheg'). Again, the 47th GvORAP was involved, swapping its Sqn 2 for a squadron of the other unit's Yak-28Rs.

The Soviet MiG-25RBs saw action in the opening stage of a conflict in which the Soviet Union was directly involved – the ten-year Afghan War. The 39th ORAP of the 73rd Air Army (Central Asian Military District), then operating a mix of Yak-28Rs and MiG-25RBs of various models, joined the action from Day One. First, on 25th December 1979 (the day when Soviet troops entered Afghanistan) seven Yak-28Rs and a Yak-28U *Maestro* trainer redeployed from the regiment's home base, Balkhash AB in eastern Kazakhstan, to Maryy-2 AB in Turkmenistan close to the Afghan border. That same day the regiment CO Col. Yuriy A. Timchenko held a briefing for the unit's MiG-25 pilots, stating that four aircraft were to redeploy to Karshi, Uzbekistan, in a few days. The deployment was ostensibly an exercise; only Timchenko and his Deputy CO Lt.-Col. Arkadiy N. Barsukov knew the real purpose (which, however, did not remain a secret too long). The 39th ORAP detachments were seconded to the Turkestan Military District whose Air Force component formed the core of the aviation of the so-called 40th Army – the Soviet contingent in Afghanistan.

Two MiG-25RBVs (coded '09 Red' and '36 Red') and two MiG-25RBSs ('12 Red' and '37 Red') were prepared for the mission; the *Foxbat-Bs* were equipped with the huge drop tanks while the *Foxbat-Ds* did not carry them, as they were to fly their missions in the stratosphere. The detachment deploying to Karshi was headed by Lt.-Col. Shamil' Sh. Mufazalov, the unit's Chief of Flight Training; it included five other pilots (Lt.-Col. Ghennadiy Shcherbinin, Maj. Anatoliy Lopatin, Maj. Anatoliy T. Doodkin, Capt. Ruslan Golikov and Capt. Andrey Dobrynin) and a 30-man maintenance team. No photo processing specialists were included – Karshi hosted the 87th ORAP whose photo processing service would handle all the pictures brought back by the MiG-25s. The ground crew and two of the pilots departed in an An-12 transport on 5th January 1980 as planned, but the *Foxbats* were held up

until 9th January by foul weather. The jets were ferried to Karshi as soon as the weather improved just enough for them to land safely – and this meant a cloudbase of 250 m (820 ft), a visibility of 2.5 km (1.55 miles) and snow. Shcherbinin flew the lead aircraft, followed by Dobrynin and Lopatin, with Doodkin bringing up the rear.

Finding accommodation for the detachment at Karshi proved to be a problem. Apart from the two resident units – the 87th ORAP flying MiG-21R *Fishbed-H* tactical reconnaissance aircraft (some of which, true enough, had redeployed to Bagram in Afghanistan) and the 735th IAP flying MiG-23M *Flogger-B* fighters, the base hosted two squadrons of 149th GvBAP (*Gvardeyskiy bombardirovochnyy aviapolk* – Guards Bomber Regiment) Yak-28I *Brewer-Cs* from Nikolayevka AB near Alma-Ata, not to mention the numerous transports staging through Karshi on their way to Afghanistan. Quite apart from the congestion on the flight line, the fighter, bomber and transport crews had taken up all available decent living quarters. The CO of the 87th ORAP allocated the newcomers a derelict building with a room measuring 3x4 m (10x13 ft) that had been a storeroom or a washroom; with much effort, this was turned into the 39th ORAP detachment's war room. The aircrews and ground crews were put up in barracks lacking any kind of amenities; on the other hand, they did not have to pay anything for this 'pig-sty' – unlike the other airmen, who lived in the local hotel that cost them two-thirds of their daily financial allowance (combat pay was unheard of in the Soviet Union). Preparations for sorties over Afghanistan began immediately; we'll let Anatoliy Doodkin tell the story:

'The detachment had two primary missions – ELINT gathering along the Iranian and Pakistani borders and PHOTINT/ELINT of designated areas in Afghanistan. PHOTINT was performed at altitudes of 6,500 m [21,325 ft] and higher; usually, however, the altitude was 9,000-9,500 m [29,530-31,170 ft]. Lt.-Col. Shcherbinin made a few sorties in the stratosphere in MiG-25RBS '37 [Red]'. Still, stratospheric reconnaissance [over Afghanistan], the way it had been done in the Middle East, was deemed inexpedient by the higher command because the enemy's air defences were not strong enough to justify such operations and because such reconnaissance was not effective enough in mountainous areas. In fairness, afterwards, when our buddies from the Yak detachment [at Maryy-2 AB] told us after the Afghan tour how it feels to be chased by an Iranian [Grumman] F-14 fighter (that particular Yak-28R was flying a reconnaissance sortie along the Afghan-Iranian border), the argument about the enemy's air defences being "not strong enough" no longer sounded so valid as it had then, in January.

Sorties from Karshi were flown in accordance with assignments received by teletype from the Air Force Chief HQ in Moscow or the Turkestan MD Air Force HQ in Tashkent. As a

Soviet technicians pose on the air intake trunk of MiG-25R '41 Blue' at Cairo-West AB.

rule, at the end of each day the Turkestan MD HQ would send us the intelligence report and combat orders. After that, Lt.-Col. Mufazalov would gather the pilots in our so-called war room, setting the tasks for the next day and reading the intelligence report to them. Next, he would announce the flight schedule, the peculiarities of specific sorties, the rules of radio exchange (the latter was kept to the barest minimum in those parts) and other relevant information. After that, the pilots who were to fly in the morning would prepare for the mission; finally, after a quick check that everything was ready, we would retire to our "royal apartments" for the night.

First call was at 6 AM, or occasionally at 8 AM (depending on when the day's first sortie was to take place), but generally we would rise early. Anyway, no more than two hours later the first MiG would be airborne. The intensity of the flights varied from one to three sorties per day to as low as a single sortie in a week. When several sorties were scheduled for the day, the intervals between them also varied; sometimes the next MiG would take off just 20-30 minutes later, while on other occasions the gap would last hours. Sorties were invariably flown with the drop tank attached, except for the stratospheric flights in the MiG-25RBSs, and lasted 1.5 to two hours. However, the routes we flew and the assignments we got were such that, as often as not, we landed with no more than 300-500 kg [660-1,100 lb] of fuel remaining – and that was "no fun" for the MiG-25, as there was not enough fuel for a go-around in the event of a missed approach. Therefore, when the aircraft were prepared for long flights, after the engines had been test-run prior to the mission the technicians would top up the fuel tanks, using the normal single-point pressure refuelling, and then open the individual tanks' filler caps and fill them all the way, using tin pails.

We wore the usual flying gear – same as back home at Balkhash: spring/autumn flight suits and flight jackets. Before the flight we were issued [9-mm] Makarov pistols (the standard sidearm of Soviet/Russian officers – Auth.) with two full clips (16 rounds – Auth.). Special load-bearing vests (dubbed "bras" by the personnel) were still unheard-of [in the Soviet Armed Forces] in those days. Also, we did not give much thought to the [Kalashnikov AKS-74U 5.45-mm short-barrel/collapsible-stock] assault rifles in our survival kits. After all, the stratospheric altitudes we flew at and our Middle Eastern experience (where the MiG-25Rs had operated with impunity – Auth.) made us a bit over-confident – which we shouldn't have been. Even though we were safe from small arms fire at those altitudes, in the event of a major hardware failure (and no-one's immune against that) we would have no choice but to punch out. One notable difference from the flights back at home was that we would leave our IDs behind. There were no explicit instructions on what to do in the event of ejection. The rule of thumb was: if you have an emergency, press on towards Soviet territory as long as you can, and if you cannot reach it, then land at any Afghan airfield. Back then, in January 1980, most of us had no clear idea of the laws and principles governing the work of the combat search-and-rescue (CSAR) service. It's just as well that we had no in-flight emergencies then – but things could have turned out differently. [...] Yet, during the sorties we always did experience an unusual feeling, a sense of danger. Radio communications were limited to the barest minimum – normally we only requested permission to start the engines, line up, take off and land. So, after take-off you would climb to the prescribed 9,000-10,000 m [29,530-32,810 ft] and head silently into the wild blue yonder. And when the DME counter would start showing a distance of 100-150-250 km [62-93-155 miles] from the base, you would realise that you were God knows where. As the figure grew, this thought would also grow on you. The radio was silent as you sailed across an endless "sea" of mountains or desert; eventually the course correction signals from the base would stop coming through, which meant you were 500-600 km [310-372 miles] away from "home". And you knew that if, God forbid, the machine should break down and refuse to glide further through the air, no-one would ever find you in this jumble of mountains. So, no matter what they might say to the contrary, you always felt a certain chill down the spine in these sorties. I cannot say for sure that **all** pilots operating into Afghanistan felt the same, but quite a few people shared similar impressions. On the other hand, when you were on your way back from the sortie and watched the numbers dwindle on the DME counter, and then finally saw the contours of your home base, it was a most gratifying feeling... I guess that's what they call bliss.

When our MiGs flew, one of our commanders qualified to control the flights of MiG-25s would join the normal ATC group on the tower at Karshi. It was either Lt.-Col. Mufazalov, or Lt.-Col. Shcherbinin, or myself.'

Maj. Anatoliy Doodkin flew four sorties over Afghanistan. His fifth sortie on 29th January 1980 in MiG-25RBV '36 Red' was cut short spectacularly and almost ended in a crash. The aircraft was carrying a full fuel load – 14,250 kg (31,415 lb) internally plus 4,000 kg (8,820 lb) in the drop tank. During the abovementioned manual refuelling procedure a technician had neglected to close the filler cap of the service tank properly; when the pilot accelerated the engines to full military power at 0945 hrs the filler cap popped under the pressure and a jet of fuel gushed out, igniting when afterburners were selected. The personnel (including the officers on the tower) watched aghast as the MiG-25 took off, trailing a 40-m (130-ft) sheet of flame – longer than the aircraft itself. Lt.-Col. Shcherbinin, who acted as ATC shift supervisor, ordered Doodkin to abort the mission and land immediately, expressly warning him not to jettison the fuel; an ejection was inadvisable because the town of Karshi was straight ahead. Doodkin was unaware that he had a fire, as all instrument readings were normal, and realised something was wrong when he smelled kerosene in the cockpit. At 0952 hrs the MiG-25 touched down. Although the fire became less intense when the afterburners were cancelled, the brake parachutes were scorched and failed to deploy, and the aircraft overran, coming to a halt some 450 m (1,480 ft) beyond the runway. Firefighters were on the scene immediately and extinguished the blaze within seconds, but the port fin and port flap were badly burnt. The culprit (who was also on the scene with the crash crew) noticed the missing filler cap and dashed back to the hardstand to get a replacement. Yet the trick didn't work; the investigators immediately discovered the deception – the shiny filler cap stood out brazenly on the scorched and soot-blackened fuselage. The technician was demoted and sent off to a unit stationed in the Soviet Far East.

In another incident at Karshi a taxiing Yak-28I bomber of the 149th BAP struck the nozzle of a MiG-25 with its wingtip. The *Foxbat* suffered no damage; the Yak-28 was worse off, being grounded for repairs for several days. Soon, however, the 40th Army command realised that the MiG-25s' capabilities were not being used to the full and it was too costly and too risky to use the *Foxbats* for missions that could easily be performed by tactical reconnaissance aircraft. In late March 1980 the 39th ORAP MiG-25s returned to Balkhash.

The MiG-25 was popular with flight and ground crews alike; the pilots liked its docile handling and willingness to forgive minor errors, while the tech staff appreciated the MiG-25's ease of maintenance. One thing the pilots disliked was the limited field of view from the cockpit because of the long nose and wide air intakes; this complicated the landing procedure because the nose obscured the runway on short finals. Pilots – especially first-timers – were impressed by the MiG-25's acceleration and rate of climb on take-off; care had to be exercised not to exceed the maximum gear transition speed. At supersonic speeds close to the aircraft's Mach 2.8 speed limit the skin would reach temperatures up to 300°C (572°F), and in the early days when the deceleration mode was not yet properly mastered, the MiG-25 did not manage to cool down adequately before landing – with the result that technicians occasionally got their hands burned.

In due course the aircraft earned such affectionate nicknames as *chemo**dahn*** (suitcase) and *gastro**nom*** (food store). While the former sobriquet was obviously derived from the MiG-25's angular and massive appearance, the other nickname was due to the fact that *alcoholic drinks* are sold in food stores – and the MiG-25P's radar and generator cooling systems contained more than 200 litres (44 Imp gal) of methanol/water mixture (in effect, vodka).

Exports of the *Foxbat* began in 1979. The slightly downgraded export versions of the MiG-25R and MiG-25RBK were acquired by Algeria, Libya, Iraq, India, Syria and Bulgaria (though the latter soon gave up using the type).

The Iraqi Air Force used its eight MiG-25RBs with some success for bombing raids on Iranian oil rigs and Tehran during the Iran-Iraq War of 1980-88. One aircraft fell victim to an Iranian Hawk missile; another was lost when an engine tossed a turbine blade, forcing the pilot to eject. One more newly refurbished aircraft crashed on landing after a checkout flight in December 1987. Soviet military experts visiting Iraq noted that Iraqi pilots were well pleased with the aircraft.

THE *FOXBAT* IN DETAIL

The following brief structural description applies to the production MiG-25RB.

The fuselage is of monocoque stressed-skin construction with 57 frames, 15 of which are main frames, plus webs, supplementary lower longerons and beams. Maximum cross-section area is 5.54 m² (59.6 sq ft).

The *forward fuselage* (frames 1-3) is made of D19T heat-resistant duralumin. The structure ahead of frame 1 is a nosecone consisting of webs/formers, stringers and skins, with a small dielectric nosecone and inset dielectric panels, and is different on various versions. Thus, the MiG-25R/RB/RBV/RBT/RBN feature a special pallet attached by six fasteners; it mounts the cameras and SIGINT equipment and can be lowered for maintenance by means of a built-in hoist. The MiG-25RBK/RBF have no pallet, featuring a longer dielectric nosecone, larger lateral dielectric panels (webs 5-7) and eight access panels; the MiG-25RBS/RBSh also lack the pallet, featuring even larger dielectric panels (web 10 to frame 1) and two access panels. The pressurised cockpit is located between frames 1 and 2, with an avionics bay beneath it. The two-piece canopy is faired into a tapering fuselage spine of semi-circular cross-section that continues aft along the entire fuselage, terminating in the brake parachute housing. The glazing is made of E-2 heat-resistant Plexiglas, mostly 12 mm (0½ in) thick. The fixed windshield has an optically flat elliptical windscreen 20 mm (0⅞ in) thick and triangular sidelights. The canopy opens manually to starboard; pressurisation is ensured by an inflatable perimeter seal.

The section between frames 2-3 is a separate subassembly connecting the cockpit section to the centre fuselage; it is a tapered oval-section semi-monocoque structure with three frames and three webs made mainly of D19T. It houses an avionics bay (with access hatches) and the nosewheel well, which is separated from the bay by a pressure bulkhead. The bay is pressurised and heat-insulated. The *air intake trunks*

(frames 2-6) are stressed-skin structures with frames and access panels absorbing part of the load. The raked air intakes are two-dimensional and have a sharp leading edge. The inlet ducts run along the fuselage sides from frame 2; between frames 6 and 7 the duct cross-section changes to circular. The flat inner faces of the intakes stand proud from the fuselage sides, acting as boundary layer splitter plates.

The *centre fuselage* (frames 3-12) is a one-piece monocoque structure welded from VNS-2, VNS-4, VNS-5 and SN-3 high-strength stainless steel. It is the primary structural element of the fuselage serving as an integral fuel tank and is divided into six bays by bulkheads. Technologically, the centre fuselage is split into the Nos. 1 and 2 tanks (frames 3-6), the No. 3 tank (frames 6-7), the Nos. 4 and 5 tanks (frames 7-11) and the No. 6 tank (frames 11-12). The mainwheel wells are located between frames 6-9. The *rear fuselage* (frames 12-14) is a monocoque structure with made of VL-1

steel. It houses the engine bays (frames 9-13) separated by a longitudinal firewall, with removable ventral cowling panels. Frame 14 carries the twin airbrakes. The upper air-brake has an area of 1.3 m² (13.97 sq ft) and a maximum deflection of 45°; the lower air-brake has an area of 1.0 m² (10.76 sq ft) and a maximum deflection of 43° 30'. The *tail-cone* riveted to frame 14 is a spot-welded and riveted structure made of steel and OT4-1 heat-resistant titanium alloy; it incorporates the airbrakes and carries the brake para-chute housing.

The MiG-25 has cantilever shoulder-mounted wings of trapezoidal planform; leading-edge sweep 41° 02', aspect ratio 2.94, taper 3.1, anhedral 5°, incidence 2°. The wings utilise a TsAGI P-44M airfoil with a thickness/chord ratio of 3.7% at the roots and a TsAGI P-101M airfoil with a thick-

This page:

Top: The nose section of a MiG-25RBS, showing the large lateral dielectric panels associated with the Sablya-E SLAR. The access panels are not fastened properly on this aircraft, which is a ground instructional airframe.

Centre: The dielectric nosecone and the main pitot, which also carries navigation/approach system aerials.

Bottom: The starboard air intake trunk.

ness/chord ratio of 4.76% at the tips. They are three-spar structures attached to the fuselage by five bolts each and made largely of welded VNS-2, VNS-5 steel and OT4-1 titanium. Each wing has two external stores hardpoints. The upper surface of each wing has a single boundary layer fence. The wingtips carry anti-flutter weights. The wing torsion boxes form integral fuel tanks. The wings have one-piece flaps and two-section ailerons made chiefly of D19T duralumin with riveted skins and a honeycomb core. Maximum aileron travel is ±25°. Maximum flap deflection is 25°; early-production MiG-25RBs had blown flaps with a landing setting of 47°.

The *vertical tail* comprises twin fins of trapezoidal planform with one-piece inset rudders. Leading-edge sweep 54°, aspect ratio 0.996, taper 4.66; the fins are canted 8° outboard. The fins are three-spar structures with internal members of VNS5 steel and AK-4 duralumin and skins of D19AT duralumin, plus dielectric antenna fairings. The fins are attached to fuselage frames 11A, 12, 13 and 14. Maximum rudder travel is ±25°. Two ventral fins of trapezoidal planform are located under the aft fuselage. The *horizontal tail* consists of cantilever slab stabilisers (stabilators), which move together for pitch control or differentially for roll control. Leading-edge sweep 50° 22', aspect ratio 3.1,

Opposite page:

Top: The rear fuselage, showing the open upper airbrake and the open brake parachute container.

Centre: The tail unit of a MiG-25RB. Note the old-style short pointed brake parachute container.

Bottom: The vertical tails. Note the different arrangement of the dielectric panels on the port and starboard fins.

taper 2.96. Stabilator travel is –32°/+13° on take-off and landing, diminishing to –12° 30'/+5° in cruise.

The retractable tricycle landing gear is fitted with twin 700x200 mm (27.55x7.87 in) KT-112/2 or KT-112A nosewheels and single 1,300x360 mm (51.18x14.17 in) KT-111/2A or KT-111A mainwheels. All three units retract forward hydraulically, with pneumatic emergency extension in the event of a hydraulics failure, and have levered suspension and oleo-pneumatic shock absorbers. All wheels are fitted with automatic anti-lock brakes. The nose unit has two steering angle limits (for low-speed/high-speed taxiing). The design of the nose gear doors varies from version to version; the only common feature is the small door segment aft of the gear fulcrum (mechanically linked to the strut). Most production aircraft have small L-shaped clamshell doors, a door segment attached to the strut to double as a mud/snow/slush guard and a narrow transverse door at the front of the nosewheel well. Each mainwheel well is closed by two tandem doors. All doors remain open when the gear is down. Two cruciform brake parachutes with a total area of 50 m² (538 sq ft) are stowed in a housing at the aft extremity of the fuselage spine, above and between the engine nozzles. The parachutes are deployed automatically on touchdown, triggered by a sensor in the port ventral fin.

Early-production MiG-25RBs were powered by two Tumanskiy R15B-300 (*izdeliye* 15B) axial-flow afterburning turbojets rated at 7,500 kgp (16,530 lbst) dry or 11,200 kgp (24,690 lbst) in full afterburner. Later aircraft were fitted with identically rated R15BF-300 engines having modified accessory gearboxes. The R15B-300 is a single-shaft turbojet with a five-stage compressor, a can-annular combustion chamber, a single-stage turbine, an afterburner and a three-position variable nozzle. The inlet assembly has a fixed spinner and 30 cambered inlet guide vanes. The compressor has an automatically controlled bleed strip aft of the third stage. A ventral accessory gearbox is provided. The engine is started by an S3 jet fuel starter with a power output of 150 shp. The starters have individual air intakes

The port wing, showing the boundary layer fence and the anti-flutter weight.

closed by doors when not in use. Each engine has an RRD-15B electronic fuel control unit. Maximum turbine speed at full military power 7,000 rpm. Engine pressure ratio at take-off power 4.75. Mass flow at take-off power 144 kg/sec (317 lb/sec). Turbine temperature 1,230° K. Specific fuel consumption (SFC) in full afterburner 2.45 kg/kgp·hr (lb/lbst·hr); cruise SFC 1.12 kg/kgp·hr.

The engines breathe through two-dimensional variable supersonic air intakes with raked leading edges having hydraulically powered two-segment horizontal airflow control ramps and movable lower lips. The forward segment of each ramp is perforated for boundary layer suction; the aft segment is fitted with vortex generators to energise the airflow. In order to minimise losses in the inlet ducts the intakes have three-position movable lower lips. The intakes are controlled by an automatic/manual control system.

The engines have separate fire warning systems and separate fire extinguishers.

The ventral fins also house aerials enclosed by dielectric fairings.

The starboard tailplane; the stabilator tips are raked for better flutter resistance.

Left: The landing gear of a MiG-25RBT.

Far left: The nose gear unit features a door segment doubling as a mud/slush guard.

Left and below: The main gear units.

Each fire extinguisher bottle holds 6.75 kg (14.88 lb) of 114V$_2$ grade chlorofluorocarbon (CFC) extinguishing agent.

The MiG-25 has conventional fully-powered flight controls with irreversible twin-chamber hydraulic actuators in all three channels. Each actuator is powered by both hydraulic systems, one system per chamber. The control runs are of mixed type, with dual cables in the fuselage spine and push-pull rods elsewhere. Directional control is provided by twin rudders powered by a common BU-190 actuator. Pitch control is provided by concerted deflection of the stabilators. Roll control is provided by the ailerons, assisted by differential deflection of the stabilators. Each stabilator has a separate BU-170 actuator, the ailerons are operated a common BU-170E actuator. The stick and pedals are spring-loaded for 'artificial feel'. Tailplane deflection is limited by an ARU-90A regulator changing the gearing ratio to prevent excessive elevator inputs at low altitude and high speed; the regulator also alters the stick forces proportionately with speed. Trimming to reduce stick and pedal loads is made by means of an MP-100M mechanism substituting for trim tabs. The MiG-25R *et seq.* is equipped with an SAU-155R1 automatic flight control system operating the control surfaces by means of RAU-107A servos.

Internal fuel is carried in 12 integral tanks – six in the fuselage, four in the wings (fore and aft of the middle spar) and (on reconnaissance versions built before the mid-1970s) two in the fins. Overall internal fuel capacity is 17,780 litres (3,911.6 Imp gal); the internal fuel load is 15,000 kg (33,070 lb). A 5,280-litre (1,161.6 Imp gal) drop tank holding 4,450 kg (9,810 lb) of fuel can be fitted on the fuselage centreline and increases the total fuel load to 19,450 kg (42,880 lb). The main fuel grade was initially T-6 grade kerosene, but ordinary Soviet RT grade jet fuel was later found acceptable.

Main 28V DC electric power is supplied by two GSR-12KIS engine-driven generators feeding separate circuits; each circuit includes a 15STsS-45B silver-zinc battery as a back-up. 200/215 V (400 Hz) three-phase AC is supplied by two SGK-11/1.5KIS (or SGK-11/1.5KIS-M) generators driven via PPO-20 constant-speed drives (*privod postoyannykh oborotov*), also feeding two circuits. The reconnaissance versions have a single-phase AC system. Part of the equipment requires 36 V/400 Hz three-phase AC; therefore, each circuit includes a T-1.5/02 transformer. If the port circuit fails, all equipment can be powered by the starboard transformer; if the starboard circuit fails, 120 V AC is supplied by an emergency PTO-100/1900 AC converter. A failure indication system is fitted and big-time power consumers are shut down automatically if a circuit fails (to ensure that enough power is available for vital equipment for at least 15 minutes during landing).

The MiG-25 has two independent hydraulic systems. The *general system* powers one chamber of each control surface actuator. It is also responsible for landing gear, flap and airbrake operation, normal wheel braking, mainwheel auto braking during gear retraction, air intake operation, nosewheel steering and jet fuel starter intake closure after engine start-up. The *control actuator feed system* powers the other chamber of each control actuator. It also caters for emergency wheel braking along with the general system. The systems use grade 7-50S-3 silicone-based hydraulic fluid. Hydraulic power is supplied by NP-70A engine-driven variable-discharge hydraulic pumps driven via fixed-ratio drives and the output is in direct proportion to engine rpm. Nominal pressure is 180-210 kg/cm² (2,570-3,000 psi). For added reliability, each system features two pumps driven by different engines; this makes sure that both systems stay operational in the event of an engine failure. Thus, the intake ramp of the failed engine remains operational, enabling a relight (unless there is a catastrophic failure and restarting is impossible).

The pneumatic system includes three independent subsystems. The *main system* seals the cockpit canopy, operates the wheel brakes, canopy de-icing valve, fuel jettison valve, generator cooling vents, brake parachute deployment/release and jet fuel starter air intake opening. It also operates the hoist for the reconnaissance equipment pallet and controls nitrogen pressurisation of the fuel tanks. The *emergency system* enables emergency landing gear extension and adjusts the intake ramps for landing. The *third system* pressurises the avionics bays and SIGINT set cooling water tank. Compressed air for all three systems is stored in bottles – 14 litres (3.08 Imp gal) in the main system, 10 litres (2.2 Imp gal) in the emergency system and 2 litres (0.44 Imp gal) in the avionics bay pressurisation system.

The air conditioning system maintains the required air pressure and temperature in the cockpit and avionics bays. It uses engine bleed air at about 400°C (752°F) and 1.1 kg/cm² (15.7 psi), which is cooled in primary air-to-air heat exchangers and a water radiator and then fed to two subsystems, one for the cockpit and one for the avionics bays, at a rate of about 240 kg/hr (529 lb/hr) and 560 kg/hr (1,234 lb/hr) respectively. The cockpit subsystem uses another air-to-air heat exchanger and a cooling turbine; the avionics subsystem has a cooling turbine installed on the starboard engine. Cockpit air conditioning air is supplied at –7°C (+19°F) and 0.45 kg/cm² (6.4 psi), while avionics cooling air comes at –20°C (–4°F) and about 0.075 kg/cm² (1.07 psi). The capacity of the air conditioning system is enough to keep cockpit temperature at 20°C (68°F).

The cockpit windscreen has ethyl alcohol de-icing.

The MiG-25 is equipped with a KKO-5LP oxygen system (*komplekt kislorodnovo oboroodovaniya* – oxygen equipment set)

The 5,300-litre drop tank is half as long as the aircraft itself. Note the aircraft's tactical code repeated on the tank.

which supports the pilot throughout the altitude envelope if the cockpit remains pressurised, or up to 11,000 m (36,090 ft) in the event of decompression. In the event of ejection the system automatically switches to the KP-27M portable breathing apparatus (*kislorodnyy pribor*) with an adequate oxygen supply for the descent. The pilot's flight gear includes a GSh-6 full-face pressure helmet (*ghermoshlem* – 'hermetic helmet') for high-altitude operations and a ZSh-5 or ZSh-7 'bone dome' helmet (*zashchitnyy shlem* – protective helmet) for lower altitudes, a VKK-6M pressure suit (*vysotno-kompenseeruyushchiy kostyum*) or a VK-3 ventilated flight suit. For over-water operations a VMSK-4 or VMSK-2M maritime high-altitude rescue suit (*vysotnyy morskoy spasahtel'nyy kostyum*), an ASP-74 lifebelt (*avareeyno-spasahtel'nyy poyas*) or ASZh-58 lifejacket (*avareeyno-spasahtel'nyy zhilet*) and a pair of gloves is provided. If the

aircraft is to operate in an NBC-contaminated environment the pilot is issued a *Komplekt*-L (Set L) NBC protection suit. The ejection seat houses a survival kit, including an inflatable dinghy, a *Komar* (Mosquito) emergency radio beacon and the usual signal flares, food ration, hunting knife, fishing gear etc.

Flight/navigation equipment includes an ARK-10 ADF, an RV-19 (later RV-18) high-range radio altimeter, an RV-4 (RV-4A) low-range radio altimeter, an MRP-56P marker beacon receiver, an RSBN-6S *Korall* (Coral) SHORAN system and a DISS-7 Doppler speed/drift meter (*doplerovskiy izmeritel' skorosti i snosa*). The aircraft features the Polyot-1I automatic flight/navigation suite including a Romb-1K automatic landing system, an SAU-155R1 automatic flight control system, an SKV-2N-1 attitude & heading reference system (*sistema koorsovertikahli*) and an SVS-PN-5 navigation data link system. Working with ground beacons, the Polyot-1I ensures automatic climb with subsequent transition to cruise at preset altitude and speed, automatic route following (using waypoints, including four airfields which can be used as staging points), automatic return to home base or one of three alternate bases, manual diversion to an airfield not programmed for the flight, auto landing approach down to 50 m (164 ft), go-around and homing in on a marker beacon.

Communications equipment includes an R-832M *Evkalipt* (Eucalyptus) UHF radio, an R-802 HF radio and an R-847RM (later R-864) HF radio. IFF equipment includes the SRO-2P (NATO Odd Rods) IFF transponder and an SO-63B ATC transponder (later replaced by the SO-69). ECM/ESM equipment comprises the Sirena-3M radar warning receiver (later replaced by the SPO-15 Beryoza RHAWS) and an SPS-141, SPS-142, SPS-143 or SPS-151 active jammer.

The mission equipment of the reconnaissance/strike versions includes A-70M, A/E-10, A-72 and S45-ARE day cameras and the NA-75 night camera (chiefly on the MiG-25R/RB/RBN/RBT), the Romb-1K SIGINT pack, the SRS-4A or SRS-4B SIGINT pack on the MiG-25RB, the SRS-9 Virazh SIGINT pack on the MiG-25RBV, the Koob-3M detailed SIGINT pack on the MiG-25RBK, the Sablya SLAR on the MiG-25RBS, the Shompol SLAR on the MiG-25RBSh and the Shar-25 SIGINT pack on the MiG-25RBF. Reconnais-

sance/strike versions are equipped with the Peleng-D navigation/bombing system (later replaced by the Peleng-DR and still later by the Peleng-DM), comprising the Anis-8 INS, the DISS-3S Doppler speed/drift meter, the TsVM-10-155 Orbita-155 digital computer and so on.

The MiG-25RB *et seq.* could initially carry up to 4,000 kg (8,820 lb) of free-fall bombs; from c/n N02022077 onwards the bomb capacity was increased to 5,000 kg (11,020 lb). The following combinations are possible: four or eight FotAB-100-80 flare bombs under the wings and fuselage (for night PHOTINT); eight FAB-500M-62 low-drag HE bombs in side-by-side pairs under the wings and in tandem pairs under the fuselage; eight FAB-500M-62s in tandem pairs under the wings and in tandem under the fuselage; ten FAB-500M-62s (either in tandem pairs under the wings and tandem pairs under the fuselage, or in tandem pairs under the wings and in triplets under the fuselage). Heat-insulated FAB-500M-62T bombs could be used instead of regular ones. Tactical nuclear bombs could also be carried.

Early MiG-25s had a crew escape system based on the Mikoyan KM-1 ejection seat, replaced by the KM-1M on late production aircraft. The KM-1M permits safe ejection at up to 20,000 m (65,620 ft) and 1,200 km/h (750 mph). It can be operated on take-off and landing at speeds not less than 130 km/h (81 mph).

Below: The cockpit of a MiG-25RBT.

Opposite page: The cockpit of a MiG-25RBF.

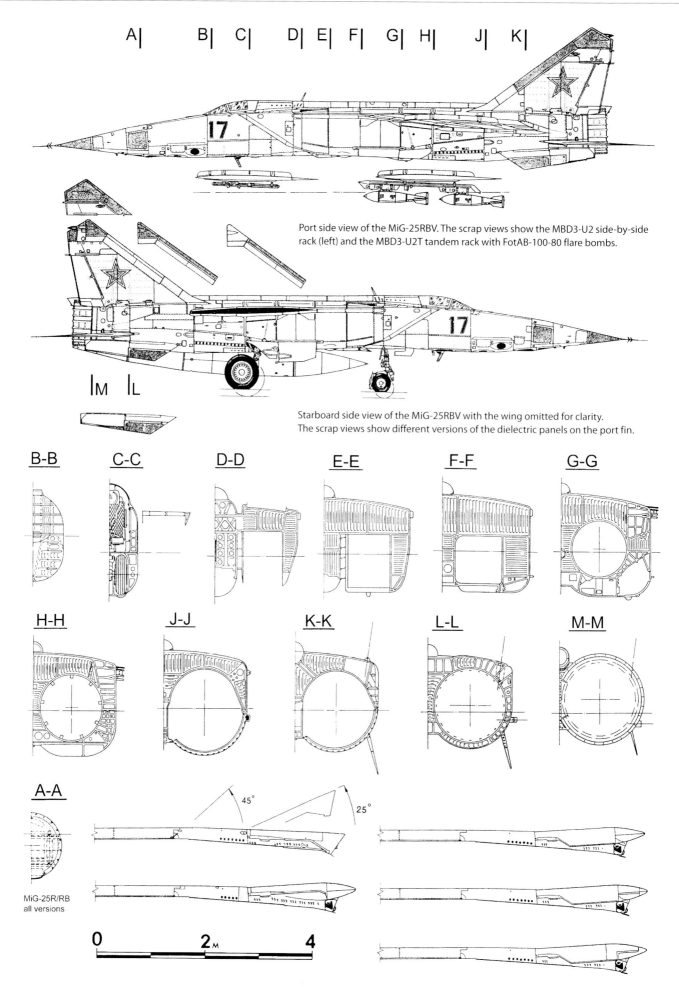

Port side view of the MiG-25RBV. The scrap views show the MBD3-U2 side-by-side rack (left) and the MBD3-U2T tandem rack with FotAB-100-80 flare bombs.

Starboard side view of the MiG-25RBV with the wing omitted for clarity. The scrap views show different versions of the dielectric panels on the port fin.

MiG-25R/RB all versions

MiG-25R/RB fuselage cross-sections and various versions of the brake parachute housing.

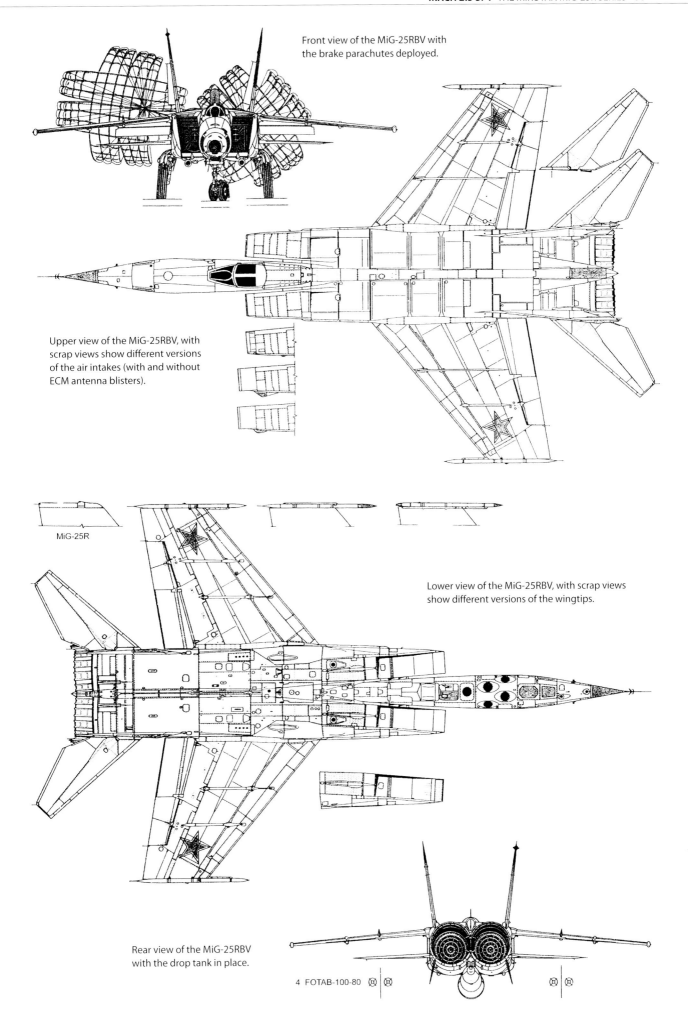

Front view of the MiG-25RBV with the brake parachutes deployed.

Upper view of the MiG-25RBV, with scrap views show different versions of the air intakes (with and without ECM antenna blisters).

MiG-25R

Lower view of the MiG-25RBV, with scrap views show different versions of the wingtips.

Rear view of the MiG-25RBV with the drop tank in place.

4 FOTAB-100-80

Left: The massive A-70M camera fitted to the MiG-25RB/RBV/RBT.

Below and right: The A-70M camera is shown mounted on its tray integrated into the forward fuselage structure; note the hoist cables.

MiG-25 BASIC DATA

	MiG-25RB	MiG-25RBN	MiG-25RU
Length, less nose probe	21.55 m (70 ft 8⅜ in)	21.55 m (70 ft 8⅜ in)	n.a.
Fuselage length	19.581 m (64 ft 2⅞ in)	19.581 m (64 ft 22⅞ in)	19.431 m (63 ft 9 in)
Height	6.5 m (21 ft 4 in)	6.5 m (21 ft 4 in)	6.5 m (21 ft 4 in)
Wing span	13.38 m (43 ft 10¾ in)	13.38 m (43 ft 10¾ in)	14.015 (45 ft 11¾ in)
Wing area, m^2 (sq ft)	58.90 (633.76)	58.90 (633.76)	61.40 (660.66)
Vertical tail area, m^2 (sq ft):			
less ventral fins	16.0 (172.16)	16.0 (172.16)	16.0 (172.16)
with ventral fins	19.55 (210.21)	19.55 (210.21)	19.55 (210.21)
Stabilator area, m^2 (sq ft)	9.81 (105.5)	9.81 (105.5)	9.81 (105.5)
Landing gear track	3.85 m (12 ft 7½ in)	3.85 m (12 ft 7½ in)	3.85 m (12 ft 7½ in)
Landing gear wheelbase	5.144 m (16 ft 10½ in)	5.144 m (16 ft 10½ in)	5.144 m (16 ft 10½ in)
TOW, kg (lb):			
normal	37,100 (81,790)	41,200* (90,830)	35,740 (78,790)
maximum	36,420 (80,290)	32,100 (70,770)	39,200 (86,420)
Top speed, km/h (mph):			
at sea level	1,200 (750)	3,000 (1,875)	1,200 (750)
at 13,000 m (42,650 ft)	3,000 (1,875)	1,200 (750)	Mach 2.65
Landing speed, km/h (mph):	290 (181)	290 (181)	290 (181)
Unstick speed, km/h (mph)	360 (225)	355 (222)	350 (218)
Climb to 20,000 m (65,620 ft), min:	8.2	n.a.	n.a.
Service ceiling, m (ft):	23,000 (5,459)	19,700 (64,632)	n.a.
Range, km (miles):			
above Mach 1.0	1,635/2,130 (1,021/1,331)†	1,865/2,400 (1,165/1,500)†	1,085 (678)
below Mach 1.0	n.a.	n.a.	n.a.
Take-off run, m (ft)	1,200 (3,940)	1,200 (3,940)	n.a.
Landing run, m (ft)	800 (2,620)	800 (2,620)	n/s
G limit	+4.5	n.a.	n.a.
Armament	4-8 x FAB-500	4-8 x FotAB-100	None

Notes: data for MiG-25RBN as carrying eight FotAB-100 flare bombs; * with 5,000 kg (11,022 lb) of bombs; † on internal fuel/with drop tank

The Modeller's Corner

ARMORY **MiG-25RB** CONVERSION KITS   1:72nd scale

When it comes to the MiG-25R/RB series, the average modeller is in for a disappointment. For some reason which the authors cannot quite understand, all manufacturers modelling the *Foxbat* have concentrated on the interceptor and, to a much lesser extent, trainer versions, while the more numerous – and equally important – reconnaissance versions have been completely ignored. Thus, the only option for the serious modeller who wants a *Foxbat-B/-D* is to build a conversion. Fortunately, latterly the Ukrainian resin kit manufacturer **Armory** has released a MiG-25RB conversion kit (Ref. No. AR-AM 72103) for a 1:72nd scale MiG-25P that includes the camera nose, wingtip anti-flutter booms and replacement engine nozzles (with photo-etched parts). The 'gooda news' is that it saves you the trouble of scratch-building the entire nose section. The 'bada news' is that the Armory kit is intended for the Ukrainian-made Condor kit (also available reboxed under the Russian brand Zvezda), which is inaccurate. ICM has a more accurate kit of the MiG-25PD but the Armory nose does not fit together too well with it, requiring copious filing and subsequent restoration of panel lines; yet, the end result is worth it. Also, the underside of the

nose features only four camera ports for the oblique cameras; the fifth camera port for the vertical camera should be on the stock plastic part of the fuselage aft of the joint line, and the modeller must remember to drill the appropriate hole himself.

In addition, Armory's range of accessories includes a replacement set of cockpit parts for the MiG-25R (Ref. No. PAV-C72061). It includes the cockpit 'bathtub', the ejection seat (with a nicely simulated harness), the stick, the instrument panel, the port and starboard consoles and the instrument panel shroud.

Above: The box top of Armory's MiG-25RB conversion kit intended for the Condor/Zvezda MiG-25P kit.

Below: The basic Condor/Zvezda MiG-25P assembled 'as is' (note the missile pylons that should not be there!) with the resin parts of the Armory conversion kit installed.

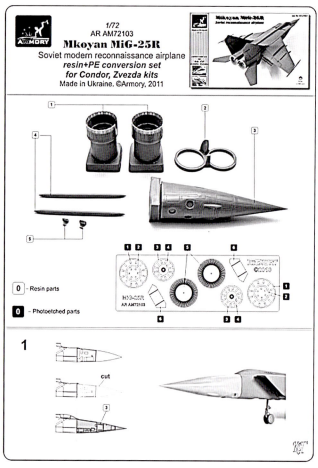

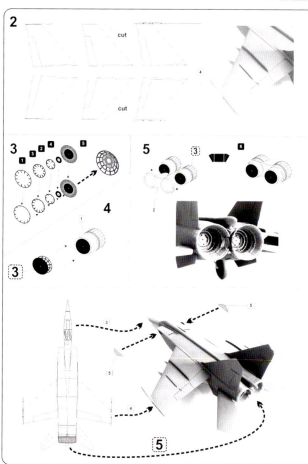

Above: The replacement MiG-25RB nose mated to the Condor/Zvezda MiG-25P fuselage. As seen, there are four camera ports; the fifth (for the vertical camera) should be on the stock plastic part of the fuselage and a hole needs to be drilled separately.

Below: The replacement engine nozzles with photo-etched afterburner flame holders and centerline fairing (in the sector where there are no nozzle petals).

Above: The straightforward instruction sheet that goes with the MiG-25RB conversion kit. Painting instructions and decals for Soviet Air Force and Syrian Air Force aircraft are included.

Above: This model of a 47th GvORAP MiG-25RBT named in memory of Soviet Air Force pilot Valentin Soogrin, Hero of the Soviet Union, is a conversion of the ICM MiG-25PD kit, using Armory's conversion kit. It was built by an author at the karopka.ru website who identifies himself as 'Denis 0102.' A proper diorama setting can work wonders!

Below: Starboard side view of the model's nose section. The camera ports are 'glazed' with Kristal Kleer or something similar.

Opposite page:

Top and centre: Port side views showing the model's nose section.

Bottom: This view gives details of the unit's combat awards and honorary appellation *Borisovskiy* painted on the nose, as well as the aircraft's individual name (with the Gold Star Medal that went with the HSU title) and the emblem of Squadron 1 on the port air intake.

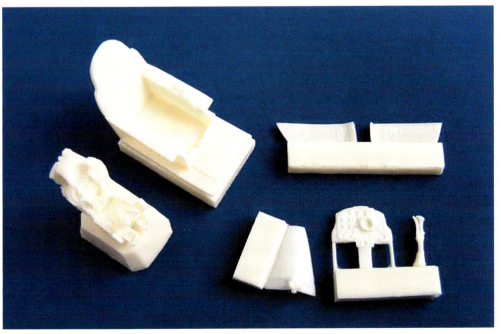

This page:

Top: Overall view of the wings, tail unit and engine nozzles. Some weathering is evident near the aileron and rudder hinges.

Above: The engine nozzles from the Armory kit look quite realistic.

Left: Armory's MiG-25RB cockpit kit in 'as is' condition.

CONDOR/ZVEZDA **MiG-25RU**   1:72nd scale

The abovementioned company Condor based in Ternopol', the Ukraine, also offers a 1:72nd scale injection moulded kit of the MiG-25RU trainer (Ref. No. C223), which is likewise sold in Russia under the Zvezda brand. Regrettably the inaccuracies found in Condor's interceptor version (especially as regards wing planform) apply to the trainer kit as well.

Right: The box art of the Condor MiG-25RU kit depicting a 47th GvORAP aircraft.

The model comes with decals by the Russian company Begemot representing a 47th GvODRAP aircraft coded '32 Red'.

Above: Zvezda's 1:72nd scale MiG-25RU built by an author at the karopka.ru website who identifies himself as 'Dimon Che'.

Below: Port and starboard views of the model's nose section. Once again, the model represents a 47th GvORAP aircraft.

Above: The centre fuselage, air intake trunks and wings.

Below: Lower view of the Condor/Zvezda MiG-25RU.

Inset: The stock engine nozzles of the Condor/Zvezda kit create a rather poor impression as compared to Armory's resin/photo-etched replacement items.

MiG-25R in colour

MiG-25RBT '55 Red', Russian Air Force, 98th GvORAP/Sqn 2, Monchegorsk. The aircraft sported the unit's regalia (left to right): the Soviet-style Guards badge, the Kutuzov Order and the Order of the Red Banner of Combat on the nose, plus the unit badge featuring a Polar owl.

MiG-25RBF '57 Red', named *Ivan Lezzhov*; Russian Air Force, 98th GvORAP/Sqn 2, Monchegorsk. This aircraft was formerly with the 47th GvORAP where it bore the same tactical code and the name *Rostislav Yashchuk*. After the transfer the old name and 'regalia' were painted out and replaced with new ones, the aircraft being christened after the local war hero Ivan Lezzhov (HSU). Later '57 Red' gained a rather gaudy camouflage. The aircraft sported the same set of 'regalia', plus the Mikoyan OKB badge on the intake.

ИВАН
ЛЕЗЖОВ

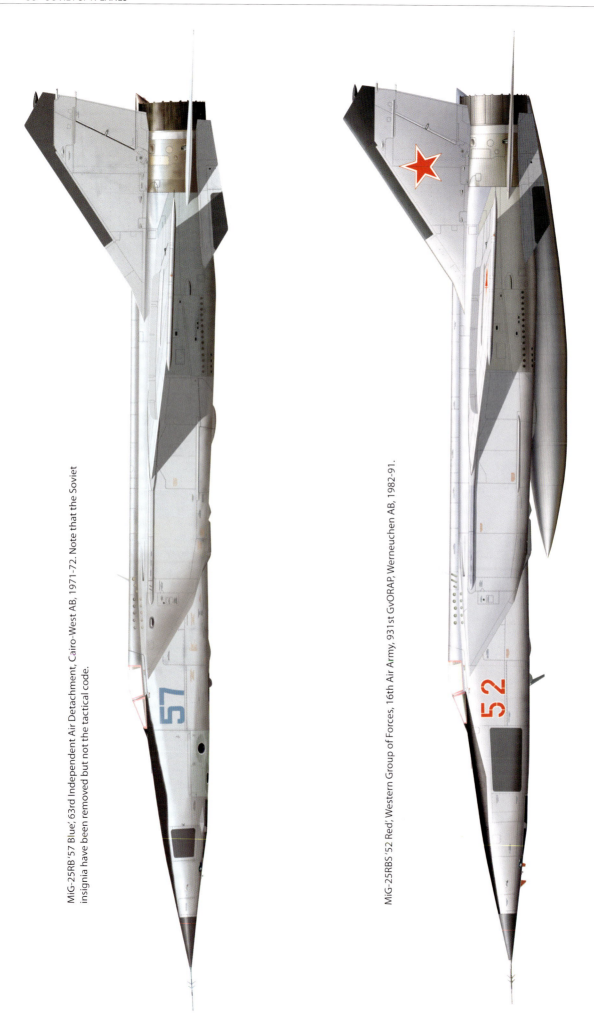

MiG-25RB '57 Blue', 63rd Independent Air Detachment, Cairo-West AB, 1971-72. Note that the Soviet insignia have been removed but not the tactical code.

MiG-25RBS '52 Red', Western Group of Forces, 16th Air Army, 931st GvORAP, Werneuchen AB, 1982-91.

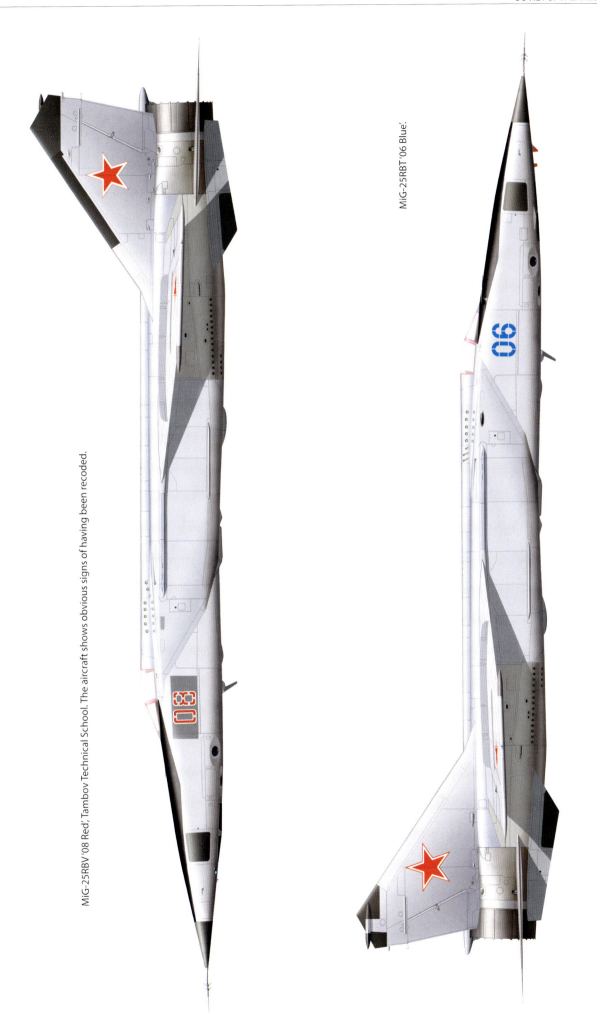

MiG-25RBV '08 Red', Tambov Technical School. The aircraft shows obvious signs of having been recoded.

MiG-25RBT '06 Blue'.

MiG-25RBT '12 Blue' with MBD3-U2T bomb racks under the wings.

MiG-25RBT '16 Red' named *Anatoliy Popov* (HSU), 47th *Borisovskiy* GvORAP/Sqn 2, Shatalovo AB. The aircraft wears the unit's regalia: the Guards badge, the Order of the Red Banner of Combat and the Suvorov Order.

MiG-25RBT '46 Red' named *Valentin Soogrin* (HSU), 47th *Borisovskiy* GvORAP/Sqn 2, Shatalovo AB. A model of this particular aircraft is featured in the book.

Starboard side view of the same aircraft; the 'regalia' were carried on the port side only.

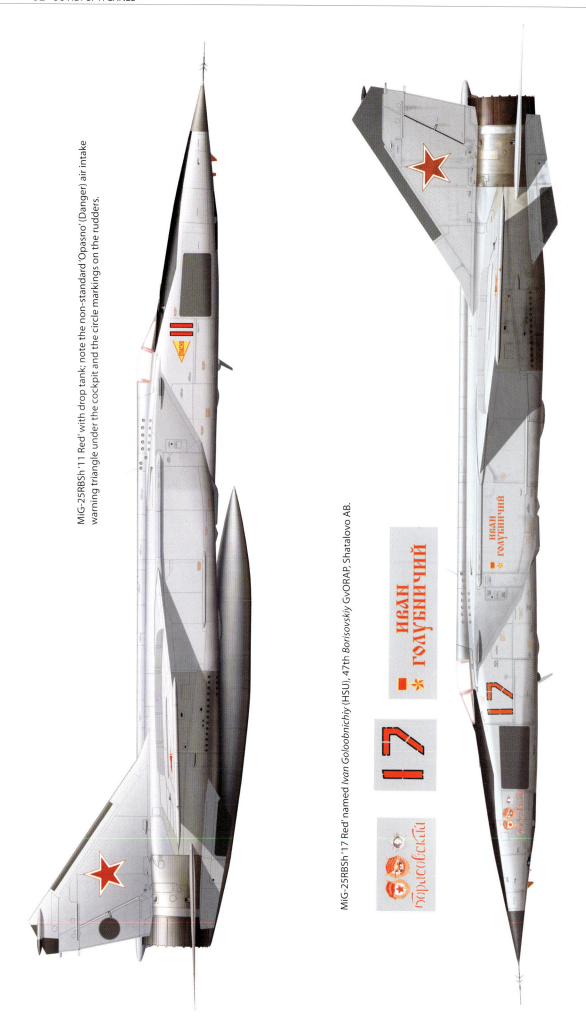

MiG-25RBSh '11 Red' with drop tank; note the non-standard 'Opasno' (Danger) air intake warning triangle under the cockpit and the circle markings on the rudders.

MiG-25RBSh '17 Red' named *Ivan Goloobnichiy* (HSU), 47th *Borisovskiy* GvORAP, Shatalovo AB.

MiG-25RBSh '41 Blue' wearing a very unusual camouflage scheme applied in the unit's maintenance shop. The paint on the tail is party weathered away.

MiG-25RBSh '76 Red', GNIKI VVS, Akhtoobinsk.

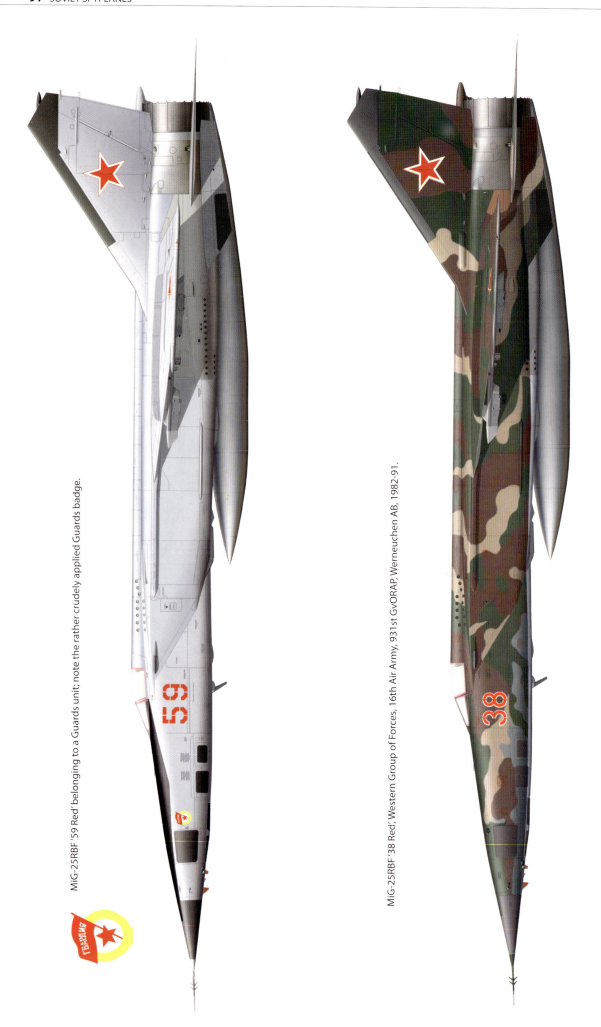

MiG-25RBF '59 Red' belonging to a Guards unit; note the rather crudely applied Guards badge.

MiG-25RBF '38 Red', Western Group of Forces, 16th Air Army, 931st GvORAP, Werneuchen AB, 1982-91.

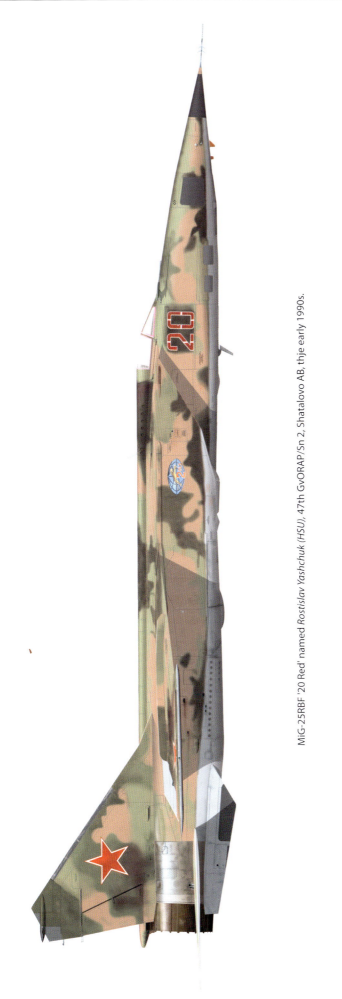

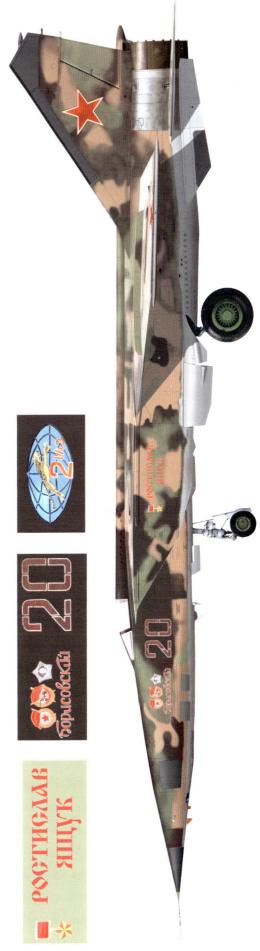

MiG-25RBF '20 Red' named *Rostislav Yashchuk (HSU)*, 47th GvORAP/Sn 2, Shatalovo AB, thje early 1990s.

MiG-25RU '33 White'.

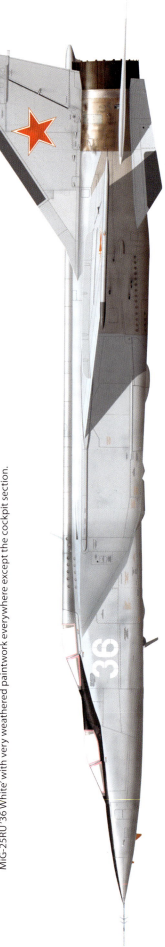

MiG-25RU '36 White' with very weathered paintwork everywhere except the cockpit section.